Callings

Finding and Following
Our Callings

Yong Hui V. McDonald

Callings, Finding and Following Our Callings
Yong Hui V. McDonald

Transformation Project Prison Ministry
P.O. Box 220, Brighton, CO 80601
www.tppmonline.org
Email: tppm.ministry@gmail.com

Published by Adora Productions.
Printed in the United States of America
First Printing: November 2016

ISBN: 978-1539849889

DEDICATION

I dedicate this book to our Heavenly Father, our Lord Jesus, the Holy Spirit, and all the people who would like to learn more about their calling and how to follow it.

ACKNOWLEDGMENTS

My gratitude to all the following generous people who helped with this book editing: Jessica Canales, Stephanie Crespin, Christopher Davis, Carol Emery, Rita Finney, Justin M. Frohna, Yvonne Garcia, Mike Goins, Julie Hillshafer, El Lisha Mayle, Fletcher McDonald, Maria Morado, David Morris, Emily Nielsen, Randy Plank, Bobbi Jo Powers, Mason Reidle, Laura Nokes Lang, Norma Rios, Sandra Robinson, Monica Rodriguez, Jared Seiders, Adam Sexon, Tito Solis, and Amber Williams. Also, I thank all who contributed their stories for this book, especially Grace who shared her email conversations with me. Thank you all for your hard work, support, and encouragement. God bless you!

I give glory to Jesus. Without him, this book could not have been written.

INTRODUCTION

On March 3, 2015, as soon as I woke up I started my daily meditation from the book, *Loving God Volume 3*. I asked Jesus which song he wanted me to sing. Before I finished my request, the Lord asked me to sing, "Lord, You Have Come to the Lake shore," which I sang for him. Then it was time to listen to the Lord, and I asked Him if He had anything to say to me. He told me to write a book on *Callings*. I asked, "Lord, you have many people who could write about callings. Why do you want me to write it?" He replied, "That's your calling!"

Almost all of my books were written because the Lord directed me to write them. If it were up to me, most of the books would not have been published. In the process of writing, I usually learn new spiritual insights, and the Holy Spirit has blessed me so much that my attitude toward writing has changed.

This book talks about the significance of what we are called to do as Christians. That is responding to God's call on our lives. We have many distractions as we try to understand our calling. I pray that you will be able to hear from the Lord what your calling is and follow your calling to glorify God.

I give glory to Jesus for this assignment. I knew this book couldn't have been written without the Lord's blessing and the guidance of the Holy Spirit.

CONTENTS

DEDICATION
ACKNOWLEDGMENTS
INTRODUCTION

Part One: Three Callings / 9

A. Our first calling – loving God / 17
    (1) Our priority and calling
    (2) How can we learn to love God?
    (3) Suggested reading
    (4) Conversations with God

B. Our second calling – Serving others / 21
    (1) Repent and forgive everyone
    (2) Open the door of your heart to invite Jesus
    (3) Eat with Jesus
    (4) Use your gifts to serve God

C. Our third calling – Live a holy life / 29
    (1) Obey the Word of God and the Holy Spirit
    (2) Develop godly habits
    (3) Resist the devil's temptation
    (4) Avoid distractions

Part Two: Stories of Callings / 37

   1. "My Dream" by Brian Young / 38
   2. "That I May Receive My Sight" By Pastor
      Anthony / 45
   3. "Finding My Calling" by Sam Rodriguez / 57
   4. "My Calling" by Iridessa Evans / 60
   5. "God's Join Project" by Douglas Purdy / 64
   6. "Suffering into Praise" by Nathan Alan
      Randall / 65

Part Three: Email Conversations on Calling / 73
               by Yong Hui McDonald and Grace Lee

Part Four: How to Respond to a Call to the Ministry / 149

Part Five: My Story of Calling by Yong Hui / 154

Appendices
   An Invitation to Accept Christ / 163
   Transformation Project Prison Ministry / 164
   About The Author

Part One:
Three Callings

Three Callings

The Bible gives examples of how God calls people and teaches us that a "calling" is God's plan and not ours. God called Moses to deliver the Israelites from slavery. This was not Moses' plan but the Lord's. Moses didn't have a clear understanding of what he had to teach the people but he learned what God wanted him to teach them: love God and love your neighbors.

God called Jonah to go and preach in Nineveh. Jonah had to decide whether he would obey the Lord or not. Jonah ran away from the Lord and disobeyed his call. He ended up inside a whale and suffered for three days. He eventually repented and responded to his call to preach, which lead to the people of Nineveh repenting and for this reason, God didn't punish them.

Jesus first called 12 disciples then later 70 disciples to preach the good news. After the resurrection, Jesus told his disciples to go and preach to all nations to spread the gospel and teach them to obey Jesus' teaching. This was God's plan and "calling" for the disciples of Jesus.

Each of us share a "calling" from God. While this is not our plan, it is God's plan, and we need to make a choice. The problem is that many people don't understand God's plans for them or how important it is for them to understand their calling.

Some people who don't understand their calling are confused and have no direction as to what they should do with their time and life. They may fall into a destructive path or waste time with insignificant things. They are not productive for God's kingdom. Many times these people feel that their life is not fulfilling but they don't understand how to have a fulfilling life.

I, too, used to be like that. I didn't know that I had a calling. In fact, I wasn't really focused on what God wanted me to do. I pursued what I wanted. In those days, my focus was only on my own well-being. I didn't have much consideration for others who were going through difficult times and were in pain. I was blind to the fact that other people needed the message of the gospel of hope and healing. I was falling into the sin of loving the world more than God. Sadly, I didn't even realize it.

The fact is that I didn't know that God had plans for my life. There was something missing. My heart was empty and I didn't know how to fill that empty spot. It took a long time for me to understand what I should do with my life. I didn't know what my calling was.

When God called me to the ministry, I was so focused on loving material things that I resisted my call. It was God's grace that helped me to change my heart as I was writing my spiritual journal, *Journey With Jesus*. Finally I made a decision to go into the ministry. My call to the ministry has been a blessing. Then after I had been in ministry for ten years, God stopped me and asked me to make a decision on what I loved the most ministry or God.

I realized that I was mixed up on what my first and most important calling was, loving God! I loved the ministry more than God for a long time. I misunderstood what it meant to love God. I thought loving ministry was loving God, but the Lord gave me understanding that loving ministry is only loving my neighbors. I am glad that He didn't let me continue to fall into the trap of ignoring Him.

The Bible teaches us the most important calling: love God and love our neighbors. In the book of Revelations Jesus asked John to write letters to seven church leaders. These seven letters teach us about what God wants from us, how we should live, what we need to change to live a righteous life, and what our callings are. Here are the letters to seven church leaders. We can learn what the Lord is asking us to do and reflect on our callings.

(1) Church of Ephesus:
"To the angel of the church in Ephesus write: These are the words of him who holds the seven stars in his right hand and walks among the seven golden lampstands: I know your deeds, your hard work and your perseverance. I know that you cannot tolerate wicked men, that you have tested those who claim to be apostles but are not, and have found them false. You have persevered and have endured hardships for my name, and have not grown weary. Yet I hold this against you: You have forsaken your first love. Remember the height from which you have fallen! Repent and do the things you did at first. If you do not repent, I will come to you and remove your

lampstand from its place. But you have this in your favor: You hate the practices of the Nicolaitans, which I also hate. He who has an ear, let him hear what the Spirit says to the churches. To him who overcomes, I will give the right to eat from the tree of life, which is in the paradise of God." (Revelation 2:1-7)

(2) Church of Smyrna:
"To the angel of the church in Smyrna write: These are the words of him who is the First and the Last, who died and came to life again. I know your afflictions and your poverty-- yet you are rich! I know the slander of those who say they are Jews and are not, but are a synagogue of Satan. Do not be afraid of what you are about to suffer. I tell you, the devil will put some of you in prison to test you, and you will suffer persecution for ten days. Be faithful, even to the point of death, and I will give you the crown of life. He who has an ear, let him hear what the Spirit says to the churches. He who overcomes will not be hurt at all by the second death." (Revelation 2:8-11)

(3) Church of Pergamum:
"To the angel of the church in Pergamum write: These are the words of him who has the sharp, double-edged sword. I know where you live-- where Satan has his throne. Yet you remain true to my name. You did not renounce your faith in me, even in the days of Antipas, my faithful witness, who was put to death in your city-- where Satan lives. Nevertheless, I have a few things against you: You have people there who hold to the teaching of Balaam, who taught Balak to entice the Israelites to sin by eating food sacrificed to idols and by committing sexual immorality. Likewise you also have

those who hold to the teaching of the Nicolaitans. Repent therefore! Otherwise, I will soon come to you and will fight against them with the sword of my mouth. He who has an ear, let him hear what the Spirit says to the churches. To him who overcomes, I will give some of the hidden manna. I will also give him a white stone with a new name written on it, known only to him who receives it." (Revelation 2:12-17)

(4) Church of Thyatira:
"To the angel of the church in Thyatira write: These are the words of the Son of God, whose eyes are like blazing fire and whose feet are like burnished bronze. I know your deeds, your love and faith, your service and perseverance, and that you are now doing more than you did at first. Nevertheless, I have this against you: You tolerate that woman Jezebel, who calls herself a prophetess. By her teaching she misleads my servants into sexual immorality and the eating of food sacrificed to idols. I have given her time to repent of her immorality, but she is unwilling. So I will cast her on a bed of suffering, and I will make those who commit adultery with her suffer intensely, unless they repent of her ways. I will strike her children dead. Then all the churches will know that I am he who searches hearts and minds, and I will repay each of you according to your deeds. Now I say to the rest of you in Thyatira, to you who do not hold to her teaching and have not learned Satan's so-called deep secrets (I will not impose any other burden on you): Only hold on to what you have until I come. To him who overcomes and does my will to the end, I will give authority over the nations-- 'He will rule them with an iron scepter; he will dash them to pieces like pottery'--just as I

have received authority from my Father. I will also give
him the morning star. He who has an ear, let him hear
what the Spirit says to the churches." (Revelation 18:29)

(5) Church of Sardis:
"To the angel of the church in Sardis write: These are the
words of him who holds the seven spirits of God and the
seven stars. I know your deeds; you have a reputation of
being alive, but you are dead. Wake up! Strengthen what
remains and is about to die, for I have not found your
deeds complete in the sight of my God. Remember,
therefore, what you have received and heard; obey it,
and repent. But if you do not wake up, I will come like a
thief, and you will not know at what time I will come to
you. Yet you have a few people in Sardis who have not
soiled their clothes. They will walk with me, dressed in
white, for they are worthy. He who overcomes will, like
them, be dressed in white. I will never blot out his name
from the book of life, but will acknowledge his name
before my Father and his angels. He who has an ear, let
him hear what the Spirit says to the churches."
(Revelation 3:1-6)

(6) Church of Philadelphia:
"To the angel of the church in Philadelphia write: These
are the words of him who is holy and true, who holds the
key of David. What he opens no one can shut, and what
he shuts no one can open. I know your deeds. See, I
have placed before you an open door that no one can
shut. I know that you have little strength, yet you have
kept my word and have not denied my name. I will make
those who are of the synagogue of Satan, who claim to
be Jews though they are not, but are liars-- I will make

them come and fall down at your feet and acknowledge that I have loved you. Since you have kept my command to endure patiently, I will also keep you from the hour of trial that is going to come upon the whole world to test those who live on the earth. I am coming soon. Hold on to what you have, so that no one will take your crown. Him who overcomes I will make a pillar in the temple of my God. Never again will he leave it. I will write on him the name of my God and the name of the city of my God, the new Jerusalem, which is coming down out of heaven from my God; and I will also write on him my new name. He who has an ear, let him hear what the Spirit says to the churches." (Revelation 3:7-13)

(7) Church of Laodicea:
"To the angel of the church in Laodicea write: These are the words of the Amen, the faithful and true witness, the ruler of God's creation. I know your deeds, that you are neither cold nor hot. I wish you were either one or the other! So, because you are lukewarm-- neither hot nor cold-- I am about to spit you out of my mouth. You say, 'I am rich; I have acquired wealth and do not need a thing.' But you do not realize that you are wretched, pitiful, poor, blind and naked. I counsel you to buy from me gold refined in the fire, so you can become rich; and white clothes to wear, so you can cover your shameful nakedness; and salve to put on your eyes, so you can see. Those whom I love I rebuke and discipline. So be earnest, and repent. Here I am! I stand at the door and knock. If anyone hears my voice and opens the door, I will come in and eat with him, and he with me. To him who overcomes, I will give the right to sit with me on my throne, just as I overcame and sat down with my Father

on his throne. He who has an ear, let him hear what the Spirit says to the churches." (Revelation 3:14-22)

After you read the seven letters, you may ask, "What is my calling?" There can be many answers from the Scriptures but I summarize in three major callings: Loving God, loving our neighbors, and live a holy life that will glorify God.

A. The first calling -- Loving God

Everyone has a calling from God and this doesn't change in any circumstances. Our first and most important calling is loving God. This isn't our plan but God's plan. When God created us, He had a purpose. Our Creator loves us deeply and wants our love. Therefore, He wants us to understand His love. His love story is the core of the gospel message.

Jesus said, "For God so loved the world that he gave his one and only Son, that whoever believes in him shall not perish but have eternal life." (John 3:16)

Jesus, a divine God, came into the world and died on the cross for our sins. His sacrifice paid for our sins and offered forgiveness so we can have a peaceful relationship with God. Our repentance and belief in Jesus Christ offers salvation and forgiveness, which is God's grace for us.

Jesus' action shows us how much God loves us. He desires to have a close and loving relationship with us. He wants us to learn how to love Him. God calls everyone to obey the commandment of love: "'The most important one,' answered Jesus, is this: 'Hear, O Israel: The Lord our God, the Lord is one. Love the Lord your God with all your heart and with all your soul and with all your mind and with all your strength.' The second is this: 'Love your neighbor as yourself.' There is no commandment greater than these." (Mark 12:29-31)

The problem of Ephesus' leader wasn't failing to serve God. He was and doing so faithfully. His problem was that he lost love for the Lord. "You have persevered and have endured hardships for my name, and have not grown weary. Yet I hold this against you: You have forsaken your first love. Remember the height from which you have fallen! Repent and do the things you did at first. If you do not repent, I will come to you and remove your lampstand from its place." (Revelation 2:3-5) It's critical that we love the Lord more than anything or anyone even ministry of the Lord.

(1) Our priority and calling

Loving God is our primary calling and it has to be our first priority in life. This is the purpose and reason why God made us. The greatest commandment is our calling. As we respond to our calling, we will be glorifying God. We each have a purpose in this life. "I will say to the north, 'Give them up!' and to the south, 'Do not hold them back.' Bring my sons from afar and my daughters from the ends of the earth--Everyone who is called by my name, whom I created for my glory, whom I formed and made." (Isaiah 43:6-7)

When people don't understand their calling, they can fall into a trap of loving the wrong people or things that the Lord wouldn't approve of. To respond to the most important call, we have to learn to develop a close and loving relationship with the Lord. When we don't have love for the Lord, loving other things and/or people, even ministry can become a hindrance in our response to the most important call—that is, loving God. When our priorities are mixed up, we can't respond to the most important call.

How can we love someone whom we can't see? We can't. We have to know him. Paul's main focus was to know Christ. Knowing Christ will lead us to understand the Father God and also the Holy Spirit's power. Paul wrote, "I want to know Christ—yes, to know the power of his resurrection and participation in his sufferings, becoming like him in his death, and so, somehow, attaining to the resurrection from the dead." (Philippians 3:10-11)

(2) How can we learn to love God?

Loving God doesn't always come naturally. We make a choice that we put God first and worship Him only. We tend to have too many distractions in our lives because we do not truly love God as we should. Jesus gives the Holy Spirit to those who love him. Jesus said, "If you love me, you will obey what I command. And I will ask the Father, and he will give you another Counselor to be with you forever--the Spirit of truth. The world cannot accept him, because it neither sees him nor knows him. But you know him, for he lives with you and will be in you." (John 14:15-17)

Jesus said he will love those who love him. "Whoever has my commands and obeys them, he is the one who loves me. He who loves me will be loved by my Father, and I too will love him and show myself to him." (John 14:21)

"Jesus replied, 'If anyone loves me, he will obey my teaching. My Father will love him, and we will come to him and make our home with him.'" (John 14:23)

One of the measures of our love is to be obedient to the word of God and obey the Holy Spirit's leading in our lives.

(3) Suggested reading

Loving God takes our commitment to know Jesus. You have to make a decision every day on how you want to know Christ and how you will obey Him. I suggest that you should start reading the gospels (Matthew, Mark, Luke, and John) to get to know Jesus, then you will be able to understand his love, the Father's love and the Holy Spirit's power.

Read the gospel as much as possible. It could be one chapter, meditate on it throughout the day, or it could be one book a day for the next 30 days. In this way you may develop a habit of learning about Jesus. Meditate on the Bible verses that speak to you every day. How much time you take to focus on the Lord and the Word of God will determine how much you can learn about God's love.

(4) Conversations with God

Your conversation with God shouldn't be a one-way conversation, so listen to God as much as possible. Your relationship with God will not be developed until you learn to give God time to speak and listen to His voice. In doing so, you will learn to pay attention to the small voice in your heart. The Lord will speak to those who patiently wait and listen. "Be still before the LORD and wait patiently for him." (Psalm 37:7)

Make a habit of praying and reading the Bible as soon as you wake up and before you go to sleep. Start a conversation with the Lord like you are talking to a friend. Ask him some questions and learn to wait. Write down your questions and ask the Lord for an answer. Don't give up quickly. Solomon gave 1,000 offerings before the Lord appeared in his dream and asked him what he wanted from God.

Practice waiting in silence for 50% of your prayer time. Learning to listen to God's voice takes time because most of the time we fill our heart and ears with too many messages. We don't give God time to speak to us. He wants to talk to us. However, we may not be paying attention to His voice. Learning to wait in silence to listen to God's voice is very critical in developing spiritual ears. In fact, many people don't understand how much God loves them because they do not listen to Him. God can speak to us in many ways but one way is to speak to our hearts in a small voice. Once you start understanding how God speaks to you, your daily calling, and vocational calling will be clear to you because the Lord wants to share His plans with you.

Prayer: "Father God, help me to understand your love for me. Help me to understand Jesus' sacrificial love for me. Holy Spirit, open my heart and bless me with a love for God."

B. The second calling -- Serving others

Our vocational calling is related to how we use our gifts. When we use our gifts to serve God, we are obeying His second command of loving our neighbors. However, people who do not know this second command are not using their gifts to the fullest to serve others.

They end up wasting the time and gifts the Lord has given them. First, we need to understand what our gifts are and that will determine the vocation that God has called us to do.

Jesus said, "I know your deeds. See, I have placed before you an open door that no one can shut. I know that you have little strength, yet you have kept my word and have not denied my name." (Revelation 3:8)

The open door is door to serve Jesus. Jesus gives us the opportunities to share him. God knows how much strength we have. We may have little strength but we can keep God's words and share our faith with others. We are called to use our gifts and help others who need to hear the message of Jesus Christ. We need to pray that the Lord will open the door for us to use our gifts to the maximum to serve Him.

How can we understand our vocational calling? Again, this starts with understanding Jesus' heart since he knows what our gifts are. Paul didn't know his calling until he met Jesus. We need to make an effort to know Jesus so we can understand our gifts. Jesus said, "I am the vine; you are the branches. If a man remains in me and I in him, he will bear much fruit; apart from me you can do nothing." (John 15:5)

To understand our vocational calling, we need to know Jesus, who he is and what he wants us to do. This is again going back to the spiritual practices of knowing Jesus. He is the key to learning how to love God and how to love our neighbors.

We can't serve Jesus without knowing him. We can't make a difference in the world or live a fulfilled life unless we make a decision to follow Jesus. Many people are wandering in the wilderness not knowing what they should do with their time and lives. They feel unfulfilled and don't know what's important in life.

The reason for this is they did not make a connection with Jesus in their life. Jesus is not their Lord and Savior. They may say he is but they are not living out that life. When Jesus comes into our life, he gives us a clear calling. He will speak to our hearts and let us know what he wants us to do. This can't happen unless you truly give your heart and life to Christ.

If you are reading this and you are agreeing that you are not connected to Jesus, I encourage you to invite Jesus into not only your heart but your life, then live and walk with him.

Many have said that they have accepted Jesus and they think they are saved. Somehow these people who have confessed that they believe in Jesus are not truly walking with him. Something is missing. That missing piece is a close, loving relationship with the Lord. Jesus said, "You say, 'I am rich; I have acquired wealth and do not need a thing.' But you do not realize that you are wretched, pitiful, poor, blind and naked. I counsel you to buy from me gold refined in the fire, so you can become rich; and white clothes to wear, so you can cover your shameful nakedness; and salve to put on your eyes, so you can see. Those whom I love I rebuke and discipline. So be earnest, and repent." (Revelation 3:17-19)

We can be deceived when we think we are doing fine but Jesus sees our hearts. We may fool ourselves but we can't fool God. Even though this person is a leader, he doesn't know Jesus. Jesus said, "Here I am! I stand at the door and knock. If anyone hears my voice and opens the door, I will come in and eat with him, and he with me. To him who overcomes, I will give the right to sit with me on my throne, just as I overcame and sat down with my Father on his throne." (Revelation 3:20-21)

There are four parts: (1) Repent, (2) Invite Jesus into your heart, (3) Eat with Jesus, (4) Use your gifts to serve God.

When we are far away from the Lord, we need to repent. What we are missing is Jesus in our hearts. Repentance is missing in many people's lives. To understand God's heart and plans for your vocational life, you have to be clean. You have to have the desire to live a life that will please God.

(1) Repent and forgive everyone

The goal of repentance is changing what we think, say, and do to please God and glorify Him. The result of repentance is a close and loving relationship with the Lord. The Scripture says, "Ask and it will be given to you; seek and you will find; knock and the door will be opened to you. For everyone who asks receives; he who seeks finds; and to him who knocks, the door will be opened." (Matthew 7:7-8)

First, go back to your early life and reflect on it and whatever you did wrong. Ask the Lord to forgive you. After this is done, ask the Holy Spirit to help you repent for one week or a month or until you break down and truly understand your sin and the need for God's forgiveness. Count the days and see how many days it takes for you to repent from the core of your heart. Here is a prayer of purification.

Prayer: "Holy Spirit, help me to repent. Purify my heart so I may understand Jesus' heart and understand what he wants me to do with my life. Show me what is right and wrong so I may live a pure life that will please God."

"From that time on, Jesus began to preach, 'Repent, for the kingdom of heaven is near.'" (Matthew 4:17) Jesus said, "I have not come to call the righteous, but sinners to repentance." (Luke 5:32)

Jesus came to earth to do God's will. That is, calling people to repentance so God will forgive them and restore their relationship with Him. "I tell you that in the same way there will be more rejoicing in heaven over one sinner who repents than over ninety-nine righteous persons who do not need to repent." (Luke 15:7)

Repentance is to ask God to forgive us for what we have done. We need to forgive everyone including ourselves. "But if you do not forgive men their sins, your Father will not forgive your sins." (Matthew 6:15)

Prayer: "Father God, I forgive everyone who hurt me and I also forgive myself because Jesus died on the cross for my sins. Please cleanse my heart and purify me so I don't fall into sin but live a life that will glorify you."

Repentance is the first step in getting closer to God. When this is accomplished, He will give you peace in your heart. If you don't have the peace of God, find whatever area in which you need to repent. We can't have peace with God without repentance.

If we are offending God with our sinful attitudes, words, and/or actions, we need to repent and change our lifestyle. Whatever you do, try to please God and not just your sinful desires. This is true repentance, not only with words but also with actions. Loving God requires obeying His words and following the Lord's command to love God and others.

(2) Open the door of your heart to invite Jesus

Jesus is not far away. He is knocking at the door of your heart everyday. He wants to walk with you and converse with you. He wants to speak to you and he wants to listen to you as well. Many lock Jesus out of their hearts though they may believe in Jesus. We tend to do things on our own and may not include or invite Jesus to be a part of our decisions. Jesus wants to communicate with you and wants to share his heart with you. You need to invite him in and not ignore him.

Here is an invitation prayer for those who have not invited Jesus into their hearts and their lives.

Prayer: "Lord Jesus, I am opening my heart. Come in and purify my heart. I confess that I am a sinner. Please forgive me. Thank you for dying on the cross for my sins. I want to love you and serve you. Teach me about your love and teach me how to serve you. Help me to understand your great love and sacrifice on the cross for me. Help me to use my gifts to serve you to the fullest for your glory. Show me what my calling is and help me follow my calling."

(3) Eat with Jesus

Many people say that they believe in Jesus but may not realize that Jesus wants to be invited into their daily lives to eat with Him. It is not physical but spiritual food we are fed by the Holy Spirit when we spend time with Jesus. Remember Jesus every day. Invite Jesus to be the closest person to you in your life and ask him to teach you about his love.

Prayer: "Lord, I invite you to be my best friend and counselor in my daily life. Feed me with your spiritual food and help me to look up to you and love you every day. Thank you for dying on the cross for my sins. Teach me about your great love and help me to love you more every day to please you. How can I please you today? What do you want me to do to please and glorify you? Speak to me so I may follow you. Teach me how to rely on you in every decision I make today for the glory of God."

(4) Use your gifts to serve God

In order to love our neighbors and respond to our calling regarding how to serve God, we need to understand who Jesus is, who we are, what we are called to do, and what our gifts and skills are.

Paul recognized his calling and responded. "But when God, who set me apart from birth and called me by his grace, was pleased to reveal his Son in me so that I might preach him among the Gentiles, I did not consult any man, nor did I go up to Jerusalem to see those who were apostles before I was, but I went immediately into Arabia and later returned to Damascus." (Galatians 1:15-17)

After Paul understood that he was called to preach, he immediately began to do so. Paul also served God while he was in prison by writing letters to the churches. In his letter, he taught people how to use spiritual gifts to serve God.

Paul said, "There are different kinds of gifts, but the same Spirit. There are different kinds of service, but the same Lord. There are different kinds of working, but the same God works through all of them in all men. Now to each one the manifestation of the Spirit is given for the common good. To one there is given through the Spirit the message of wisdom, to another the message of knowledge by means of the same Spirit, to another faith by the same Spirit, to another gifts of healing by that one Spirit, to another miraculous powers, to another prophecy, to another distinguishing between spirits, to another speaking in different kinds of tongues, and to still another the interpretation of tongues. All these are the work of one and the same Spirit, and he gives them to each one, just as he determines." (1 Corinthians 12:4-11)

You may be called to preach, teach, clean the church or show hospitality. These are all ministries for the Lord. Anything that is related to serving God is our vocational calling. A vocational calling can change at times but whatever you do for the Lord is your vocational calling at that moment.

When we love God and try to follow Him, He gives us the gifts of ministry. The ministry I am talking about is not just being a spiritual leader or pastor but anything we can do to serve God with our gifts. Whatever we do, when we use our gifts to honor and please Him, we are responding to our calling.

Prayer: "Lord Jesus, help me to understand my gifts so I can respond to my call to serve you."

Sin is not just doing something wrong, but not doing a good thing as well. James wrote, "Now listen, you who say, 'Today or tomorrow we will go to this or that city, spend a year there, carry on business and make money.' Why, you do not even know what will happen tomorrow. What is your life? You are a mist that appears for a little while and then vanishes. Instead, you ought to say, 'If it is the Lord's will, we will live and do this or that.' As it is, you boast and brag. All such boasting is evil. Anyone, then, who knows the good he ought to do and doesn't do it, sins." (James 4:13-17)

When Jesus talked about a parable, he spoke of a master who gave five, two and one talents to different servants. Those who received five and two talents worked hard and multiplied what they were given were rewarded. "His master replied, 'Well done, good and faithful servant! You have been faithful with a few things; I will put you in charge of many things. Come and share your master's happiness!'" (Matthew 25:21- 23)

When a servant who received one talent hid it and didn't use it, he was rebuked. "His master replied, 'You wicked, lazy servant!'" (Matthew 25:26)

We all have received different gifts and talents from God. The most precious gifts are life and time. We need to use our time to love and serve God with our gifts and talents.

Prayer: "Lord, Jesus, reveal your plans for my life so I can understand my gifts and serve you. Bless me with spiritual wisdom, knowledge, understanding, and revelation so I can love you and serve you with my gifts and be obedient."

C. The third calling – Live a holy life

We may say that we love God and love our neighbors by using our gifts to serve Him. But if we don't show it with our actions by living a righteous and holy life, we are not following our third calling. "Make every effort to live in peace with all men and to be holy; without holiness no one will see the Lord." (Hebrews 12:14) Holy living is a kind of living that we need to pursue and that starts with cleaning our minds and hearts from all impure thoughts and desires. We do this by repenting and keeping our hearts focused on God. Even when we say that we love God and we use our gifts, if we live in sin, we can't please Him.

David loved God and he used his gifts to serve God but he sinned when he committed murder and adultery. God punished David for his sins. We need to ask God to forgive us but after we are forgiven, we need to live a life that will honor God by living a righteous life.

We need spiritual guidance to live righteously as Christians. To do this we need God's help from the Bible. It's very critical for us to understand the Bible so we have God's values and know what is right and wrong. To live a holy life, we need to: (1) Obey the Word of God and the Holy Spirit, (2) Develop godly habits, (3) Resist the devil's temptations, (4) Avoid distractions in life.

(1) Obey the Word of God and the Holy Spirit

Jesus has given us the gift of someone who will guide our path. He said, "And I will ask the Father, and he will give you another Counselor to be with you forever." (John 14:16)

We have a divine counselor and that is the Holy Spirit. He will guide us if we are open to listening to him.

Prayer: "Holy Spirit, purify my heart so I will know what is right and wrong. Help me to choose to live a righteous life that will please the Lord. Teach me how to love God and others by using my gifts. Help me to make good decisions on how to live a life that will honor God."

Choosing good friends will influence you with pure thoughts and a godly life. Paul warns us about people whom we spend time with. "Do not be misled: 'Bad company corrupts good character.' Come back to your senses as you ought, and stop sinning; for there are some who are ignorant of God-- I say this to your shame." (1 Corinthians 15:33-34)

Choose to find friends who can guide you to God and a righteous life. We need to rely on the Lord to find righteous friends.

"Trust in the LORD with all your heart and lean not on your own understanding; in all your ways acknowledge him, and he will make your paths straight. Do not be wise in your own eyes; fear the LORD and shun evil." (Proverbs 3:5-7)

God told Joshua, "Be strong and very courageous. Be careful to obey all the law my servant Moses gave you; do not turn from it to the right or to the left, that you may be successful wherever you go. Do not let this Book of the Law depart from your mouth; meditate on it day and night, so that you may be careful to do everything written in it. Then you will be prosperous and successful. Have I not commanded you? Be strong and courageous. Do not be terrified; do not be discouraged, for the LORD your God will be with you wherever you go." (Joshua 1:7-9) God told Joshua to know the law word of the Lord and meditate day and night, and obey it. To live a pure life, we need to know the Scripture and listen to God's voice and obey it daily.

(2) Develop godly habits

Without daily spiritual discipline, we may fail to respond to our daily callings. In everything we do we need to ask, "Is this going to glorify and honor God? Would it please Him? Am I using my gifts to serve God? Is this a pure thought and action?" If our focus is sincerely responding to our call to love God, He will reveal to us what our vocational calling is. After all, we can't understand God's heart or His plans for us until we start getting closer to Him and listen to His heart. Without the Holy Spirit's help, we miss out on serving God and purifying our heart. To respond to our call, we need to develop a habit of devotional life. Here are some suggestions: As soon as you wake up, pray to show God how much you love Him.

Prayer: "Father God, I love you. Lord Jesus, I love you. Holy Spirit, I love you. I thank you for giving me this life. I ask you to help me to love you more today. Thank you Jesus for dying on the cross for my sins. Guide me so I can use my gifts to serve you. Help me to live a life that will glorify you. Please tell me if there is anything that you want to speak to me."

Worship God every day by giving thanks for what He has done for you and how He has blessed you. Then ask the Lord to lead you and bless you so that the Lord will help you to do the things that will please Him.

Read the Scripture to learn about God's heart, especially Jesus' heart, by reading the gospels. Meditate on the Scripture or inspirational stories that touch you throughout the day. This will help you focus on loving the Lord.

Listen in silence and continue listening throughout the day by praying, "Lord, I am listening. If there is anything I need to know, please speak to me." This will help you develop an open heart for the Lord. The more you practice silence and listening to the Lord, the more you will recognize His voice.

Prayer: "Lord, Jesus, help me to obey your word so I can live a life that will please you and honor you. Help me to develop a habit of loving you so I can serve you according to your will and not my will."

(3) Resist the devil's temptation

Our mind is a spiritual battlefield. There are four voices: the Holy Spirit, the devil, our voice, and other people's voices:

(1) God's voice, which is the Holy Spirit speaking to us so we can follow His ways to live a holy life.

(2) The devil's voice are the thoughts and the voices that give us suggestions on how we can fall into sin and temptation. That makes us fall into misery and torment.

(3) Our voice, which is our thinking. Yes, we have a sinful nature so we can make wrong decisions and can fall into sin without the devil's tempting us.

(4) Other people's voices are the things we may remember from what others speak to us and also external influences through books or the media.

We need to be careful to follow the voice of God so we can live a holy life. The book of James talks about wisdom that comes from God and also from the devil. "Who is wise and understanding among you? Let him show it by his good life, by deeds done in the humility that comes from wisdom. But if you harbor bitter envy and selfish ambition in your hearts, do not boast about it or deny the truth. Such 'wisdom' does not come down from heaven but is earthly, unspiritual, of the devil. For where you have envy and selfish ambition, there you find disorder and every evil practice." (James 3:13-16)

"Submit yourselves, then, to God. Resist the devil, and he will flee from you. Come near to God and he will come near to you. Wash your hands, you sinners, and purify your hearts, you double-minded. Grieve, mourn and wail. Change your laughter to mourning and your joy to gloom. Humble yourselves before the Lord, and he will lift you up." (James 4:7-10)

Our sinful desire can lead us to fall into sin: "When tempted, no one should say, 'God is tempting me.' For God cannot be tempted by evil, nor does he tempt anyone; but each one is tempted when, by his own evil desire, he is dragged away and enticed. Then, after desire has conceived, it gives birth to sin; and sin, when it is full-grown, gives birth to death. Don't be deceived, my dear brothers. Every good and perfect gift is from above, coming down from the Father of the heavenly lights, who does not change like shifting shadows. He choose to give us birth through the word of truth that we might be a kind of first fruits of all he created." (James 1:13-18)

4) Avoid distractions

Mostly, we follow our sinful desires instead of focusing on loving God, however, there are many distractions in life that are beyond our control. We need to have God's wisdom to know what they are and avoid them when we can. David was distracted when he looked at a beautiful naked woman. He should have recognized that this would bring disaster to his life and affect his relationship with God, but he didn't resist sin. In fact, he continued with his sinful plans to commit murder by trying to cover up after committing adultery. If David handled distractions in life by obeying the commandment "Do not commit adultery" and "Do not commit murder," he could have avoided so much grief, loss, and humiliation. He misused his position of authority instead of caring for the people God had entrusted to him. This did not please the Lord.

Joseph, unlike David, ran away from temptations from a woman who was his master's wife. He said, "My master has withheld nothing from me except you, because you are his wife. How then could I do such a wicked thing and sin against God?" (Genesis 39:9)

Joseph's concern was not just people. He also wanted to live a pure life before the Lord. We need to recognize the distractions that hinder us from loving God and loving our neighbors.

Paul listed many distractions in our life and said, "But mark this: There will be terrible times in the last days. People will be lovers of themselves, lovers of money, boastful, proud, abusive, disobedient to their parents, ungrateful, unholy, without love, unforgiving, slanderous, without self-control, brutal, not lovers of the good, treacherous, rash, conceited, lovers of pleasure rather than lovers of God--having a form of godliness but denying its power. Have nothing to do with them." (2 Timothy 3:1-5)

We may see from the outside that we love God and love others. It's easy to fall into the sin of loving ourselves and not considering what God wants us to do. In this life, we have many distractions. Not only do we need to keep our hearts pure and treat others with love but also we have an obligation to teach others how to love God and love others.

In addition, we must recognize distractions in life and avoid them by avoiding ungodly people, music, media, books and anything that promotes impure thoughts and actions so that we may live a life that glorifies God.

If we fail and fall into sin, we should repent and turn to God for forgiveness. David didn't do that until the

Lord sent the prophet Nathan to confront him with his sin, waiting about a year. Let's not wait if we have sinned. Let's repent and make a change right away so we can learn to live a pure life. "If we confess our sins, he is faithful and just and will forgive us our sins and purify us from all unrighteousness." (1 John 1:9)

Prayer: "Lord, Jesus, please help me to repent all my sins. Help me to understand your heart."

Conclusion

Can we be lovers of God? I believe we can. We need to obey the word of God and learn and practice what the Holy Spirit is asking us to do and respond to that calling every day.

Can we love our neighbors by using our gifts? Yes, we can, by being considerate, caring and kind to others according to God's will.

Can we live a pure and godly life? We can by obeying the word of God, relying on the Holy Spirit's leadership and by obeying Him daily.

Loving God, loving others, living a pure and righteous life has to be our daily focus. If we do that, we will be responding to our callings which will be in turn, glorify God.

Part Two:
Stories of Calling

Stories of callings

1. "My Dream" by Brian Young

In my dream I was walking through a forest of olive trees. As I passed through the forest, I saw a crystal clear river. It looked like there were diamonds in it. I walked to the edge then I started to walk into the river and to the other side. It was so deep, it came above my head. As I came out of the water I saw a tall set of staircases in front of me. I climbed the stairs and I began to become younger the higher I climbed. When I reached the top of the stairs, I was a baby. Then I saw someone sitting on a throne. I could see a man's feet up to his chest, but there were clouds over the rest. Then he reached down and picked me up and set me on his lap. He asked me what I wanted. The words that came out of my mouth were, "I want a servant's heart."

He said, "It is given."

Then I heard loud cheers and when I looked around, there were soldiers with swords and shields as far as my eyes could see. He sat me back on the stairs. As I began to walk back down on the stairs I turned back as an adult. About seven soldiers followed me to help me back through the water and to the forest. This dream came to me years ago when I first accepted Jesus into my life. It seems like yesterday I can still remember it. I pray to God to show me what it means. About ten years later in 2012, I had another dream that I will never forget. In my dream, someone gave me a gold watch with a diamond on it. I took it to the jeweler and he told me it was a very expensive and rare watch. He wanted the watch but I kept it and left the store.

As I was standing outside someone else came to me and gave me a pair of gold keys to a gold car. They all had the same letters engraved on all three keys. Everyone that saw them was amazed and asked me where I got them. They were shocked when I told them a stranger gave them to me.

I never saw the person who gave them to me, only a hand placing them in my head. This dream stayed on my heart until I finally asked two people whom I trusted. God would give me answers through them. Chaplain McDonald and Pastor Liebert. I have spent nearly seven months behind bars.

I had a bad childhood. When my Dad returned home from Vietnam shell shocked, he suffered from alcoholism. He beat my mom. I often woke up at night to the sounds of this abuse. Although my mother was not interested in church she forced me to attend religiously. I resented the going to church because of it. When I got older I pursued a career in the family business as a chef, in New Orleans, Louisiana.

I was born in New Orleans in a part of the city called the 9th Ward, the area hit hardest by Hurricane Katrina and still being rebuilt today. A couple months before the hurricane, I had just moved back to New

Orleans from Ohio. I had recently backslid, because
I met someone who partied a lot. We were trying to live
right so I decided to move to New Orleans with her.
That's when I started experimenting with drugs. I always
drank prior to me being saved, but I had never used hard
drugs like cocaine. The Holy Spirit told me one day to
choose who I was going to serve, at the time I was going
back and forth with God.

One day we got a call from my girlfriend's mom.
She said she was coming to visit us and take us back to
her new farm house in Moore, Oklahoma. She came and
picked us up and we drove straight back to Oklahoma.
We stayed there for about 2 weeks. Then I was ready to
go back home, and we were preparing to do so, but we
saw on the news there was a storm in the Gulf of Mexico.

I didn't pay too much attention to that and we
headed back to New Orleans. The storm soon turned
into a massive hurricane, and they named it Katrina. I still
wasn't too worried, but the closer we got, the worse it
was. What I saw in August, 2005 was the most disturbing
I have ever seen. Houses were being blown away.
People were screaming, children were lost, people were
being swept out to the Gulf because the Mississippi River
had rerouted through the city.

That wasn't the worse that came. After the
hurricane had gone, dead bodies were floating in the
water, and some were eaten by the Louisiana wildlife.
People were hungry and babies were crying. It was a
lawless time where robbery, stealing, rape, and all sorts
of crime happened. The police abandoned their post, the
jails let prisoners go. It was hell. FEMA and the
government help didn't come for a couple days, but the
church was there from day one. It was almost as if the

city was quarantined because when people were trying to enter other cities, they were told at gun point to go back. Babies, pregnant women, and the elderly were told the same. We were not allowed to go back into our homes.

Later they called us to evacuate. Every part of my childhood and family history was totally gone. It seemed as if the world and God abandoned the people of New Orleans, but in my heart I can hear God say, "I will never leave you and I love you." (Psalm 136:1-26). His love endures forever and nothing will separate us from the love of God.

At the time, because of all the sadness and hurt, I didn't want to believe that and that was the beginning of my hell. I was a very successful chef, but when Hurricane Katrina hit, I lost my home and job. I turned away from God and turned to drugs and alcohol and an immoral lifestyle. From August 2005 to April 2012, I wondered why God would let this happen. I never got an answer because I was so wrapped up in trying to put my life together.

I have been to a few rehabs in between those years, but didn't complete any of them. I always left early thinking, "I can do it myself. I don't need God." I was told to get help for my PTSD but I didn't. Recently I got into trouble and I was arrested and placed at Adams County Detention Facility. I couldn't believe I was arrested for this crime and I felt lost. Prior to this, I've never been to jail or prison and had any problem with the law except minor traffic violations.

I cried out to God and asked why is this happening, but didn't get an answer. I started reading a book in the dorm called *Four Voices*. It told me to write out questions for God and fill it in when He answers. Also, it explained how God speaks in many ways.

I wrote ten questions I wanted to ask God. He answered all but one, and that question was, "What do you want me to do with my life?" A few days later, a voice spoke to me and said, "Feed my sheep." I got mad because I was in jail.

"How can I feed your sheep with an attitude?" I am housed in F2400 and I slept for the first couple days. One day the Holy Spirit said, "I haven't left you. Feed my sheep." So, I got out of my bed walked around the pod and saw about five people reading the Bible. They were all Hispanic guys. Surely, God was not speaking to me to join this group. I didn't know how to speak Spanish.

One of the guys invited me to sit with him. His name was Pedro. He spoke some English. I sat down and listened to them read aloud in Spanish. I just followed along with my Bible. Pedro asked me to explain to him about a verse they didn't understand about salvation. I replied it is a gift from God and you cannot earn it, but it is a gift.

He translated back what I said in English. From that point on, I began to teach the Bible study group every day. More people started to come to study and the pod was united for one hour a day studying God's Word.

Slowly my attitude started to change. Hurricane Katrina was a bad time in my life. I am still healing from the loss of family members and my own addictions. It may sound strange but I would have to say, "Thank you God for the storms in my life."

I now realize I can't go back to the old lifestyle. According to Jeremiah 29:11, God has plans for me. "'For I know the plans I have for you,' declares the LORD, 'plans to prosper you and not to harm you, plans to give you hope and a future.'"

The guys sometimes ask me to explain something to them and I sometimes think to myself, "I am not worthy to teach His word anymore as I am an ordained minister that's in jail. I'm ashamed of that." But God tells me in a quite gentle voice, "Feed my sheep."

It will be seven years on Aug 25th, 2012 that I ran from God just like Jonah did. Now, however, I am running to God. I am willing to be his bond servant to go into the world to preach the gospel. "They overcame him by the blood of the Lamb and by the word of their testimony." (Revelation 12:11a)

The joy of the Lord returned to my heart. Nothing else has mattered since then. Prior to my backsliding, hands were laid on me early in my ministry before Hurricane Katrina. I was to reach the world through Jesus, and become a missionary.

God actually brought the world to me because while in this jail, I have been ministering to people from Sudan, Somali, Mexico, South America, and Russia. Some received Christ into their lives, and some haven't. But they still heard the gospel.

I began to be hard on myself and think I had wasted my life like the Prodigal son. I was in here on a 16-32, 10-32, 10-32, and 1-3 sentences, which for me at 42 years old, basically is a life sentence. I am innocent of these charges, yet I put myself in a position to be charged for them. I was mad at myself for not doing God's will for my life and wasting the gifts He gave me for His glory. I cried, prayed to God for forgiveness, and I asked for justice. I have served Him and if that means to go to prison to teach and preach the gospel there, I will go. To make a long story short, justice has been served, and I will be released early in October 2012.

I was amazed with how God blessed me with ministry even though I had turned away from Him. He forgave me and welcomed me back home. I made a vow to God not to give up on following Him no matter how hard it gets. Even when I fall, I will get back up and continue to follow Him. I have a desire to go into the entire world to preach the gospel, to feed the hungry, and to heal the broken hearted with the help of the Holy Spirit. After I received all the signs, I still had doubts if God would use me in a mighty way. Then God gave me a new dream, and I finally got the answers for my questions and doubts.

Chaplain McDonald said the car in my second dream represents God's approval of my ministry and that I am called to the ministry. It brought tears to my heart because the Holy Spirit spoke to me at that moment and said, "I restored you."

Then Pastor Liebert came to visit me a day later and said to me, "Here is what the Letters ESP mean: 'Special ministry of Evangelism and Missionary,' and that God had spoken to me and said, 'Now is the time to serve God, step out in faith that you are being led by the Holy Spirit to do this good work.'"

The things I used to do in the world such as drugs, fornication, partying, etc., I now hate because God has restored me back to Him. Even though I don't feel Him close to me or working in my life, I now know it's not about how I feel. It's about what I believe. He said, "I will never leave you nor forsake you and nothing will separate me from the love of God which is in Jesus."

"Thank you God for giving me my life back and welcoming me back home."

2. "That I May Receive My Sight" by Pastor Anthony

The story of my calling can be compared to the story of the blind man, Bartimaeus, whom Jesus healed from (Mark 10:46-52). As an inmate with pending court dates, months apart, and a large bail amount; I often begged for Jesus' mercy. As I write now, I have been here for five years. Ironically, about three weeks after being in C mod - pod 3, another inmate, 'G' started a prayer circle. He seemed passionate, dedicated, and had conviction. He led the prayer circle for about three days; but then he was reclassified, and moved.

I had just received a Bible, and was immersed in it, to say the least. After 'G' left, I decided to inquire of the POD rep, 'Bo', if he thought it was a good idea to continue the circle, and if he would mind if I led it. Bo thought it was a good idea, and wanted to help; so we continued the circle by reading *Daily Bread* passages every day. Bo began each day's circle; and afterward, I would read verses from the Bible, tell a bit of my understanding of them, and then ask for prayer requests.

Next, I would pray for Jesus to grant each prayer request along with a general prayer, and we would end in reciting the 'Our Father Prayer.' We also always shook hands with each other before we parted. Praise God for giving me the strength, courage, and wisdom to take on this calling.

Before my arrival, Bo had already done at least a year of a two-year sentence. When I met him, he was a stick of dynamite with a short fuse and a big voice. As time went on, not only could I see Jesus working on myself, but I could also see an awesome change in Bo and other inmates. Observing these changes in each inmate and in myself, along with the many answered prayers, brought joy to my soul. For me, I can relate to Mark 10:49, which says, "Jesus stopped and said, 'Call him.' So they called to the blind man, 'Cheer up! On your feet! He's calling you.'"

Every night as I studied the Bible for scripture to present to the other inmates that would relate to our plight in general and strengthen our fellowship, I prayed to Jesus to guide me and to allow the Holy Spirit to speak through me. I didn't have the insight or seminary education needed to be confident in my new found jail house ministry. So I sought Jesus even more, and cried out to him for understanding, and that he would be my eyes. I didn't want to stumble. I didn't want to mislead others, as a blind man leading the blind. Without the mercy and grace of Jesus, I would have fallen into a pit. Jesus asked me, "What do you want me to do for you?"

Like Bartimaeus, I replied, "That I may receive my sight." Immediately, I began attending Chaplain's worship services and bible studies eight to ten times per week. One pastor, Rick Anderson, taught the Bible in a very scholarly fashion. He gave vast insight into Bible history, with an emphasis on belief and faith in Jesus.

Another pastor, Chaplain Wayne Bracket, brought in many very insightful books, like *Mastering the New Testament* by Earl Palmer, *Insights into Bible Time and Customs,* by G. Christian Weiss, *The Handwriting of God,* by Grant R. Jeffrey, and various other books. At one point, I was almost written up for having too many books in my cell! I had 20 at least, all Bible history and/or Christian books. I actually even had a book titled, *Am I Called?: The Summons to Pastoral Ministry* by Dave Harvel. I started a dictionary of Hebrew and Greek words that I learned, and was able to earn a beautiful New King

James Version Study Bible by memorizing 1 Corinthians Chapter 13. I could have never understood how blind I was, until I asked Jesus for my sight. Jesus brought me all the tools and wisdom and strength to honor His name and give Him absolute glory.

As time passed, and prayers were answered for many inmates, my faith grew stronger. For one inmate, we prayed that his infant baby girl would be returned, and that she would be healed, and that the inmate would be given a sign that she was all right. His baby had been given to people on a Native American Reservation in South Dakota to be cared for because his wife had been arrested after being forced to drive a wanted murder suspect from Colorado to South Dakota.

We prayed for three days. On the third day, he was able to get a hold of the grandmother who had arrived in South Dakota to look for the child. She had found his infant daughter, and was bringing her back to Colorado.

In the prayer circle, we prayed for the health of family members who had afflictions. We prayed for court dates to go well, and we prayed for an inmate to be able to get his daughter back from Adams County Social Service Department before she was adopted. The next day, he was called for a hearing to do just that. Then his public defender visited two months in advance, and informed him he would be getting help with housing and finances as soon as he was out. This would allow him to gain full custody of his daughter. With the exception of a few prayers, all were answered. As time has passed, I have been able to see the presence of Jesus in peoples' lives.

One of my cellmates, an Apache Native American, spent three months with me, and had to endure countless conversations and sleepless nights as we discussed the Bible and Jesus. As a Native American, he had very grounded beliefs; and although he heard many stories about the Bible, he regarded Nature as supreme. He was a gang member from a gang similar to the one that I grew up in. He is only twenty years old, and has already become accustomed to gang life, and is pretty jail savvy. I can relate with many of his life experiences, and felt it was my duty to help him change and come closer to God. As we talked and shared life stories, we noticed how evident it was that Jesus brought us together.

He began coming to the prayer circle, and we prayed for his younger brother, who was going to be undergoing liver transplant surgery. He was waiting to be bonded out so he could be there for his brother at the hospital. His court date was scheduled for a month after the surgery, on his brother's birthday.

I explained God's timing and faith. He was bonded out Christmas Eve, just a few days before the surgery's set date, and left believing in Jesus. While here, he had attended services and Bible studies with me very often, and was able to leave with a Bible and some Christian books.

He had called me 'Pastor five Head' while he was here because of my big forehead. I am pleased to say that he has written me. Many inmates have said they would attend my church, including my former cellmate. I am thankful to be able to say that because of the Bible studies and the presence of Jesus, there have only been a couple arguments lately, and they have ended peacefully. Before the Bible studies, tempers flared and violence ensued.

I have had the privilege of attending the services of seven pastors/chaplains in this jail on a regular basis. (Rick Anderson, Wayne Bracket, Vanessa, Chaplain McDonald, Bill Strong, Al Agnew, Pastor Joe, Chuck, and the "old Christian guy who just likes to read the Bible.") I have enjoyed the wisdom they shared and I'm proud that they all give glory to Jesus for their wisdom. I have taken bits and pieces from them all, and utilized them to continue our prayer circle.

I recently began to notice how insightful I have become. My general knowledge of Scripture, both of the Old and New Testament, has been described as advanced and extraordinary. Jesus has healed my blindness. When I was blind, I could see nothing. However, after Jesus tested my faith by allowing the tower to lock us down during many prayer circles, and warning us to be quiet, I cried out all the more, "Lord Jesus guide me and strengthen me. Be my eyes and my ears and allow me the ability to discern your word and to convey it to others."

Minister means, 'servant', and I have found great joy in serving, even from jail. We hold our prayer circle next to the workout equipment, and trust me, Jesus has given me more strength than any amount of push-ups or pull-ups can. I have learned to stop praying for selfish desires, like being released from jail by some miracle. I have learned that everything happens according to God's will, and have begun to ask Jesus to guide me where he needs me. While I have always been considered very intelligent and a great orator and linguist by my peers, I now realize that God doesn't want me to be a genius. He wants me to be prepared to understand what he inevitably wants to teach me.

When memorizing 1 Corinthians 13 to earn my Bible, I learned that this Scripture was there to prepare me to love. Matthew 22:36-40 says, "'Teacher, which is the greatest commandment in the Law?' Jesus replied: 'Love the Lord your God with all your heart and with all your soul and with all your mind.' This is the first and greatest commandment. And the second is like it: 'Love your neighbor as yourself.' All the Law and the Prophets hang on these two commandments."

Also, the story of how Jesus washed the disciples' feet (John 13:12-17) shows the greatest example of the sincere love and the joy He had as a servant. The important thing to know is that love is not weak, and Jesus was not weak. Love is strong; and not only is Jesus strong; He also gives strength to the weak.

In my time at Adams County Detention Facility, the Lord has helped me change the hearts of three atheists. One in particular was an eighteen-year-old guy who began by leading the "Our Father Prayer" in the prayer circle, and left here having memorized a few verses that meant a lot to him. He was homeless and yet he left with a Bible and a smile after we read, 'The Whole Armor of God' (Ephesians 6:10-18). We have done this for all of the men who are being released.

I believe that I have been called by Jesus. Just two days ago, I introduced myself to an older man who had become my 5th cellmate. He jumped up on the top bunk and went straight to sleep, as did I. In the morning, I woke him for 'chow' at 4:30 am. Afterward, he went back to sleep, and I let him sleep in as I cleaned the whole POD alone as it was our scheduled day to clean. I then slept for a bit and he sat at a table alone.

After lunch, I worked out and periodically stood in a

sunbeam that shines through a window near the pull-ups bar, while he paced back and forth in front of me. We caught each other's eye a couple of times. When we locked down at noon, he went straight to bed and I read the Bible, but we didn't talk. I could tell he was pretending to sleep and maybe listening to my breathing to see if I was sleeping.

For some reason, I decided to take a nap, and I must have fallen asleep pretty quickly. Later, I awoke to the sound of him gasping for air and choking. I lay on the bottom bunk afraid to look because from the sound, I could tell it was going to be bad. I thought he may have tried popping his neck or something and hurt himself. I called to him but he didn't answer. I finally rolled out of the bunk and saw his face with his tongue hanging out. His face was plumb red, his eyes were popping out of the sockets, and a sheet tight around his neck. Guilt filled my heart instantly and the first thought that entered my head was that I hadn't taken the opportunity to talk to him about God.

I pushed the emergency button, the door popped and I ran to the Tower to summon help. After the deputies made sure he was okay, and took him away, all I could think of was my missed opportunities to 'save him'. I still think about this. One deputy said I did save his life that day.

However, now I know God used me to save his life, so that he can use someone else to help save his soul. All I could think about was, "I could have ministered to him." That's how I know I was called.

My next cellmate came just hours later, and I wasted no time talking about Jesus. He opened up to me a lot, and though he was an admitted atheist, he attended the prayer circle the next day. Praise God that I was able to reach out to this man.

I was raised in east Denver and lived most of my adult life in that area or downtown. I once had a loft on the 16th Street Mall when my children were four and five years old. I was very proud of that, considering I had been kicked out and homeless since the age of 12. I put myself through high school, and went to the Colorado Institute of Art for Computer Animation and Graphic Design. I was a pretty wild teen, and I have been a gang member, consumed alcohol, and smoked weed since I was very young.

God was always protecting me and refining me. God opened many doors for me and shut many others. The Lord brought many amazing people into my life yet none more meaningful than my own children. When I had my daughter at age 22, my entire life changed.

I went from working jobs to owning a Graphic Design Company and from working for a small business and corporation, to designing for them. I also helped build businesses for friends.

At age 23, I had a son. My two oldest children have always been my best friends. I actually prayed for God to send them to me and He did. I often talk about God to them, and teach them many stories and passages from the Bible. I taught them how to pray, and let them know that if I was not able to be there for them, they should know that the Lord always will be.

Inmates have often asked me if I have always believed in God or if it was just from being locked up. The truth is, I have always believed in God. I just only spoke to him with my children and my family. When I was 32, ten years after my having daughter, I had my last child, a son. I haven't seen him since he was nine months old, and he is now four. I pray that someone is teaching him how to pray, and conveying the "Good News" of the Gospel to him. When I was four, I lost my grandmother to a heart attack. A few days later, she visited me in a dream. Ever since that day, I have believed in God.

In my 36 years, I have had hundreds of what I would call divine occurrences happen to me. Enough occurrences to fill volumes, however, the point is God has always been speaking to me, and preparing me for ministry.

At some point, I had to realize that it wasn't enough to just teach my children and talk to my family about God. God really wants to use us all to minister to each other and to glorify His holiness at every moment.

Honestly, the more you begin to understand that God created all things and manipulates all happenstance for our best interest, the more you want to thank God and give him the glory for everything that happens in your life. 'On the outside', my family and friends know me as a genius, an artist, and a father.

In here, people call me pastor, and I explain that there is nothing better than to know Our Lord Jesus Christ. Many inmates have thanked me for my prayers and help. I give God the glory, but they still insist on thanking me.

I tell them to thank God instead, and to accept Jesus into their lives, as I have. I tell them that they will know then that we all have the power to pray, and that according to our faith, God is the greatest gift we can receive. I also say that the Lord Jesus Christ shall be the greatest minister we will ever know.

Like Bartimaeus, I asked Jesus for my sight, and He replied, "Go your way, your faith has made you well." Immediately, I received my faith and followed Jesus on the road. The Lord has helped me accomplish many awesome things in my life.

Nothing has brought more joy than sharing the Word of God and observing the change in people. At first I thought, "Who am I?" I am nothing more than an inmate and sinner just like everyone else here. Then the Lord said to me, "You are my child. Go and tell the rest that they are also. Share with them my word and my love."

"Thank you, Lord, for allowing me a part of this fellowship and family. Please guide me and strengthen my spirit, in your mighty name, Lord Jesus, I pray. Amen."

Having been called by God, my ultimate goal is to honor him and glorify Him every minute of every day. I believe that I have been chosen to discern, interpret, and convey the Word to others in order to bring souls to Christ through the Gospels.

This is truly the greatest gift of grace and rich honor bestowed on an individual. To know that God not only forgives your sins and accepts you into his family and kingdom, but also finds favor with you and asks you to bring others with you to Christ.

For the first time I am empowered to share the Word, I shall do so with the blessing of Jesus and the grace of God. I will do all I can to build the church with a diverse array of individuals.

Other areas that I would like to work on with individuals on are the Arts, Physical Training, and furthering their education in STEM categories. Basically, I feel it is quite feasible to help people strengthen their mind, body, soul, and spirit with emphasizing on praying to Jesus, glorifying God, and incorporating scripture into everything that interests them because our talents and abilities are only by the grace of God.

Along with all of this, it has been a lifelong goal of mine to find a way to put many fruit trees in public parks and also expand the urban garden programs. Many people have told me that my dreams are not possible; however, I know that all things are possible with God. (Luke 18:27)

I discovered long ago that God has built into me innate tools and talents that I have been able to utilize and build businesses with. I am also able to network people and resources to create and benefit many non-profit groups.

Although I have put together many benefit shows for battered women's shelters and homeless in general, I never did it to glorify God or to preach the gospel. Yet, I have found that the greatest gift you can give to someone in need is a relationship with our Lord and Savior, Jesus Christ.

I would love to begin as soon as physically possible to build a church from the ground up. I understand that to begin my ministry with a strong foundation, I need to find a church that has already begun to establish itself with the same relationship and goals in Christ that I have.

I would love to find a church that loves the Lord and is committed to God and His word, and one that also wants to expand and reach a diverse demographic group of soul-searching Christians. I can see myself helping to establish a network of many churches to help involve God in everything they do. This network can support their needs and refer individuals to places in the communities to help sustain their work. Jesus is, was, and always will be the sustainer in their walk. He was able to build the confidence in his apostles as well as heal those who were born blind, deaf, mute, and lame.

Jesus built many churches through his disciples and was able to have the word spread to the world. I believe that it is possible to network believers and to bring them together as the great family of God with all the glory going to His Holy Name. I thank God I am able to participate in this divine fellowship and am reminded of 1 John 1:1-7.

"Lord please continue to guide me and build my path straight so I don't have to wonder which way to go. I pray for the courage to take the first step until my last breath. Amen."

"I have been an artist all of my life. I am blessed to be able to follow the path the Lord Jesus has shown me and to use my talents to glorify His name, especially behind these walls. Romans 12:21 explains my goals: "Do not be overcome by evil, but overcome evil with good."

Chaplain McDonald's books are a true blessing. To have the opportunity to work with her for the glory of Jesus Christ is an answered prayer. Halleluiah.

"Therefore, my dear brothers, stand firm. Let nothing move you. Always give yourselves fully to the work of the Lord, because you know that your labor in the Lord is not in vain." (1 Corinthians 15:58)

Anthony Perez is a father, graphic designer, poet and painter. He shows his work in Colorado galleries and in the historic Westminster Arts District of which he is also the designer of their logo. He also illustrates and has been published in various other context. He drew all the illustrations for *Journey With Jesus Four: The Power of the Gospel.*

3. "Finding My Calling" by Sam Rodriguez

After eight months at ACDF I find myself not as an inmate but a chaplain's assistant and a book editor. These are two jobs or paths in life I never once thought of myself doing. It's amazing how a situation that started out negative became something so positive.

This simple experience has opened my eyes and my mind to a place I didn't see before and probably never would have. I'm thinking of writing a book myself or even a few books, who knows. I just know that I want to surround myself with situations and people that are positive.

All this came about because I was moved to a trustee position here in ACDF and immediately assigned to be a chaplain's trustee. I didn't have a whole lot of relationships in my life growing up so I didn't know what my involvement would be in this new job.

Was I going to have to read the whole Bible and start doing multiple prayers daily, or make some kind of drastic change in my daily habits that I didn't do before? I wasn't worried but I was curious as to how much this new job would force me to do something I haven't done.

What I found out was something so much greater than my petty curiosity. After meeting Chaplin McDonald, I quickly found out that I could participate as much or as little as I wanted, whatever I felt comfortable with. My job was to simply assist the chaplain with anything she needed.

I would help with setting up tables and chairs, setting up communion. I can pick out some books so that the people who would come to service could take them when they left. Also, I handed out the very fun and uplifting song sheets. Almost every service began with music. The sheets were there so you could sing along if you wanted to. Many of the songs have such a good beat to them that many of the people would move to them or dance, if you will. This could even mean moving your head or tapping your foot. What I soon discovered was awesome.

Every person I met or saw was smiling and happy and if they weren't at the beginning of the service than they were by the end of the service, or at least in a better place mentally. Over six months I got to meet and see so many different people that were in a very negative place and became very positive even if it was only for a small amount of time. Nothing else mattered in that hour that we were all together. Not age, race, or social status; everyone was positive.

The next thing you know, I was enjoying going to work. I was even starting to sing more confidently every day. No way! I figured out right away that Chaplin McDonald was the very same person who wrote or was responsible for the many books that were available for us. And so as I dug a little further I found out that she has been doing this for many years.

I felt kind of honored that I was the one that was assisting her with quite a few of her services. Then one day she asked me if I was good at grammar and if I could tell her if this was the correct way a sentence should be worded. I looked at it and told her that it wasn't and I think that it would go more like this.

She said thank you and that's what she thought and it sounded better also. Soon after she told me that she was busy writing more books because God asked her to and would I be willing to look at what she had wrote, and adjust any errors that I may find. I was happy to. I knew that I had a pretty strong educational background and good grammar, punctuation and spelling was something my mother was always adamant about.

After doing my first editing project, I quickly saw how happy she was that I caught things and fixed them. I also learned that there were many people that helped her with her books. There were quite a few people here in ACDF that helped with editing and contributed almost all the drawings in her books. Once again I felt honored that I was contributing to chaplain's great cause. She was very appreciative of all my help.

Now here I am helping make books matter and I feel like I am a semi-pro book editor. I never thought for a second that I would someday do that. In the six months that I was a chaplain's assistant, I have seen every emotion possible from the many people that I was around every day. From anger to happiness, tears to laughter, sometimes from the same faces every week.

All I know is that people who were coming to Chaplin McDonald were generally very positive and happy to be there, including myself. To find something so positive in such a negative place is truly awesome; it's something I want to stay with me for the rest of my life. Good follows good and positive follows positive. That's something that I can look forward to doing the rest of my life.

4. "My Calling" by Iridessa Evans

God gave me a calling when I was a little girl. At the age of 11, I was living in North Carolina on Pope Air Force Base. My stepfather was in the Air Force and we found out that he had to go to Honduras for a whole year.

That was a hard year for my mother. She had my grandmother come from Colorado to live with us that year. I remember one night I had my friend come and spend the night with me. We decided to sneak out of the house and had a bottle of whiskey and took eggs and egged cars. The next day my friend had to run and tell the whole neighborhood about what we had done. There had been another girl that was mistaken to be my friend and she got in trouble and ended up showing up to my house. I then had to tell my mother the truth. My mother, of course, lectured me and said, "You need to get your little life together and pray."

I thought, "Hmm, pray? I've never done that." I then went to my room and grabbed my book of Bible stories. After reading up to David and Goliath, I got tired, got on my knees and prayed, "God, if you are really there, can you show me?"

I went to sleep and I saw a very bright, bright light come towards me. I woke up and sat wandering what it was, then went back to sleep. I work up again and I saw nothing, then I went to sleep. This time there was a caress on my face and I woke up startled yet again. I remember feeling at peace; I wasn't scared. We had a night light in the hallway and I looked at my door. Underneath it, I saw a shadow slowly walking by. I knew it was Jesus, letting me know He is real.

From then I have strived for Jesus, hoping that I see him and talk with him. So I just started praying and studying His word. It was motivating. However, I didn't have a close relationship with my parents and lost faith. I prayed, wondering where God was. He never came to see me again. I thought He gave up on me.

I had my first child in 1997. I was happy I had a family of my own, until, my son's father started to abuse me. After I had my second son, I started using drugs heavily for the first time. One night I was getting high on cocaine and drinking Seagram's 7 and I was led to read the Bible. I read the Book of Matthew and remembered crying uncontrollably.

I felt selfish; I fell to my knees crying out for Jesus to forgive me. Then when I went to open the Bible to continue reading the end of Matthew, I saw in big black letters, "Do not drink alcohol or use drugs." I went to show my friends the next day and the letters were gone.

After that, I didn't want to touch alcohol or drugs. I kept striving to find my walk with God. I was finding out my purpose, but then met a guy who took that from me. I know I left God for a while, but soon had a dream that Jesus was teaching. I was reaching out to him but I kept drowning in the water.

I woke up and knew God was telling me what was going on. I was losing my perseverance. We had two beautiful children, but their father was mentally abusive. Years later I left him. I then began to go to church again, feed the homeless, and minister unto others, before allowing my loneliness to overtake me again. Then I got in trouble, lost my kids and everything. I ended up in prison.

I thought God had given up on me while reading my Bible; God put me to sleep for a moment. I was a little girl sitting in an empty room. I had on blue jeans and a pink jacket. I had pigtails in my hair and I called out "Father, Father." In the doorway God approached it and said, "I'm here." It was a very large showdown in the doorway and His voice was deep. I woke up to see my Bible pages were moving, then there stopped and it looked as if a finger was holding the page. God spoke through Isaiah 47:8-15 and then told me to read all of Isaiah 48. I fell to my knees because of the things that were spoken to me about losing my children, and some of the things I did as a child and how they affected me to this day.

Isaiah Chapter 48 told me to change my life for what God would do for me. I asked, "God what is it that you want me to do." Later on, I had a dream I led a lot of people into a house. There were all kinds of tornadoes. I had them go away then all of a sudden a big tornado came and made the other tornadoes disappear. When I woke up, I wondered if that was my calling to lead people. God then spoke to me through Joshua 1:6-9.

I just got regressed and put back in jail from the halfway house. I allowed the world to distract me. I just found out I'm pregnant here at the ACDF. My write up was something I didn't do, but God told me, "Iridessa, you have a calling in your life. It's my precious jewels that I lock up in a box," and that was how I let Him minister to me.

Since being in D Module, I have ministered to others, and prayed with others. We have started a Body of Christ group in our pod. We study, pray, worship, and are at peace. God has blessed so many women in here and we have seen so many miracles, it amazes me how God works.

I now am preparing myself for my walk with God.

My boyfriend knows of my relationship with God and knows how God is number one in my life and encourages me to keep going. We now pray on the phone together every night with a baby girl on the way. I'm supposed to go back to State prison, but pray that I don't, hoping to go to the Haven where I can have my child.

One night I got anxious. I told God, "I'm tired." Sometimes I wish I could be the one who is ministered to. I help others and I feel you are not there." So, God said, "Read *Journey With Jesus*." I asked, "What?" He said it again. So, I read *Journey with Jesus* and He told me to read Lamentations, and Isaiah 54. I cried and cried. The book helped me so much that I said, "Okay God, help me be an awesome leader for your people." I contacted the chaplain and asked her for *Journey With Jesus Two*. She didn't have it but had *Journey with Jesus Three*. I then understood that God was preparing me for spiritual leadership. I laughed and thought how God is good.

Don't give up. We all have gifts and a calling in our life, but we need to prepare. God has an army that has come together. Don't be overwhelmed or give up. Know that our blessings are unseen or are around the corner. Keep running the race until you are at the end. God is building His army. We can all come together and fight the unseen spiritual forces that are out there to save our brothers and sisters. God will never leave you or forsake you. Sometimes it will seem that He is not there, but He is, and that is when He is carrying you. God bless you. God told me to start my own ministries called, "Foreknowledge" meaning the knowing of something before it happens.

5. "God's Join Project" by Douglas Purdy

Working as an inmate volunteer on editing for the chaplain McDonald and TPPM has most definitely been a positive experience for me. It has brought me closer to God, helped me feel useful in an environment that engenders feelings of despair and uselessness, and helped me to use some of my gifts to serve God.

Editing materials for Chaplain has brought me closer to God. I have a graduate-level education (graduated from Metro State, Summa Cum Laude, Master of Professional Accounting), and I enjoy reading a lot. Since I read so quickly, I spent a lot of time reading secular materials for the first couple of months that I was at ACDF.

Once I began editing for the chaplain, I had a steady supply of Christian material to peruse (and correct, re-read, re-hash and fix up). I estimate I have spent an hour plus each day the past few months immersing myself in spiritually uplifting literature. This has led me to read other inspirational books and to participate in a couple of Bible correspondence courses as well. Spending more time with God, both in the work I have been doing and in prayer, has been one positive outcome from my association with TPPM.

Editing materials for TPPM has also helped me to feel useful in a jail environment that has a tendency to propagate feelings of distress, despair, and uselessness. Editing books also helped me participate in something positive in a negative place. I know that my work has had an impact, and that the additional future impact is that souls may be won to Christ as a result of this joint effort.

If my work has made something more readable or understandable, it just makes these materials that much more powerful in their goal of sharing Christ with others. As I recently got sentenced to a halfway house, I have been dealing with internal feelings (which I now rebuke as the devil's voice!) of "I don't think I'm good enough to succeed" and "I'm a failure because of my past mistakes."

I know that this isn't true! God uses all things for the good of those who trust in Him. (Romans 8:28) I am thankful for the opportunity to use this bad situation, incarceration for Good (editing Loving God 1, 2, 3, *Journey with Jesus 3*, *Four voices (children's version*), and *Women Who Lead*, a grant proposal, and a research proposal). I know that besides the positive impact on me, this work will have a positive impact on others in the future (though I may not see the effects myself.)

Editing these materials has helped me to use some of my gifts to serve God. Before I came to ACDF, I was definitely not using what God gave me for good. I am extremely thankful to have had the opportunity to get myself right with the Lord and to start over - rededicating myself to Christ and serving Him as best I can. Working with Chaplain and TPPM has been a definite blessing. I am glad that God brought me together with this wonderful program. I am a new man because of the changes God has made in my life. He has used TPPM's book projects to initiate some of His miracles. My life will be forever different for the experience.

6. "Suffering into Praise" by Nathan Alan Randall

During my time in prison and out on parole, I fully understood why my life was the way it was. I had made awful mistakes and hurt people that were around me and

I was paying for the life I had led up to that point.

But nothing could prepare me for what was to come. I was blind-sided and unprepared to face the circumstances which I now face. My life was turned upside down and I was broken hearted. Little did I know that in the midst of my problems and struggles laid a plan of comfort, love and forgiveness, a plan in which I didn't expect yet a gift I didn't expect to receive. God had a plan and calling to a man who was once one of the worst sinners.

"Here is a trustworthy saying that deserves full acceptance: Christ Jesus came into the world to save sinners-- of whom I am the worst. But for that very reason I was shown mercy so that in me, the worst of sinners, Christ Jesus might display his unlimited patience as an example for those who would believe in him and receive eternal life." (1 Timothy 1:15-16)

When I was arrested on September 16th, 2010, I was in a state of shock. I had no clue why I was being arrested or why the parole department was treating me with such a hostile attitude while I was being arrested. It didn't make sense to me and it took several weeks before I even knew why I was being held in jail.

At first I kept my cool and figured at the most I was under investigation and that I would be released after a few weeks. I was being held at Denver County Jail and the officers ran warrant checks for me and nothing would show up. I knew my arrest was a mistake and that I'd be out soon.

I ran into several of my prison friends and I shared with them how good I was doing out there. I told them how much I had done for myself and how I was keeping out of trouble and off the parole radar. I gave myself all the credit and was so sure that I would be back out. I told my friends this was just a small bump in the road.

Several weeks later I met with my parole officer and she explained that I had a few 'technical' violations but the main issues were the felonies I was being charged with out of Adams County. I was troubled in my heart, and my mind was racing off the chart.

My exalted attitude and confidence in myself was gone. I broke down in front of my parole officer and began to cry and ask questions. I didn't know who, what, when, where, or why.

"For whoever exalts himself will be humbled, and whoever humbles himself will be exalted." (Matthew 23:12) Shortly after this meeting with my officer, I was transferred from Denver County to Adams County. I faced the judge for the first time and slowly I learned bits and pieces about my case and why I was in their custody. I didn't fully understand my circumstances until I had my discovery report in my hands.

I started to reach out to friends and to a loved one. But to my surprise I was left with only a few true friends and a few family members for support. Everyone had deserted me. In my despair I grew frustrated, angry, and bitter. I wanted to scream and yell. I wanted to fight and break something. Here I was alone, and facing a lot of time for something I had done, all because I made someone jealous and they wanted to hurt me by calling my parole officer.

And now, all the people I loved and trusted who said they loved me were jumping ship at the first sign of trouble. What I didn't understand was it was God at work in my life. God was preparing me for His plan and He knew that I had friends and family in my life that would be a stumbling block to my relationship and walk with God.

A lot of the people I reached out to had caused me a lot of pain in my life, but they were all I had. God hardened their hearts so I would be free of the snares their relationship were in my life. He was making room in my life for Him and for Christian brothers and sisters.

In my helplessness and distress God gave me peace and comfort. For the first time, I didn't lash out and allow myself to be consumed in my anger. Instead I picked up a Bible and grasped my faith in Jesus Christ.

I had lived an awful life before prison and while I was in prison, I just wanted peace in my life. I had wanted to find the answer to why my life was so out of control and I knew I could no longer fix my life myself. I needed God to fix not only my life, but me.

The very first day in general population, I was invited to an unofficial Bible study in the pod. I accepted and started to participate in fellowship with other Christians as well as attend Chaplain's Worship, and a Bible study led by a great man named Chuck. He took time out of his life to spread the good news to the Maximum Security inmates.

My life here in Adams County was being transformed. I had a hunger to study the word of God and I was seeking God and I found out that before I was seeking Him, God was seeking me.

"And we know that in all things God works for the good of those who love him, who have been called according to his purpose. For those God foreknew he also predestined to be conformed to the likeness of his Son, that he might be the firstborn among many brothers. And those he predestined, he also called; those he called, he also justified; those he justified, he also glorified.

What, then, shall we say in response to this? If God is for us, who can be against us?" (Romans 8:28-31)

God gave me strength in my time of need. He encouraged me through others. He taught me and spoke to me through the Scriptures and through His servants. I stood up big before others to share what God had put on my heart. A love that does not fail and a relationship that does not end. I prayed for a church to attend when I was to get back out and He answered that prayer faithfully. God placed a good Christian lady in my life, Pastor Barbara. She had a heart for us inmates in jail and prison. She visits inmates here and writes to us. She became a source of guidance and encouragement for me. God was slowly replacing the people He had removed from my life.

God blessed us with another day of worship in our cell house. He brought us a minister who we could relate too and who didn't sugarcoat anything. She reached us by telling us about herself and the way God worked in her life. God blessed me with a dream team of men and women who loved God and who had a heart for people in low places.

I accepted Jesus Christ as my Lord and Savior, and asked him to come into my heart. I confessed with my mouth that I was a hell - deserving sinner who was guilty and lost. I believe that Jesus came to earth to die as my substitute on the cross, and that He rose again from the dead. He died not only for my sins but for all the sinners all of this world. This Jesus is my personal Savior, my Lord, and my king.

About ten months into my arrest I made the choice to be baptized. By faith I was saved from the fires of hell, but now I made public expression of my faith that I was a member of God's family. I am a child of God.

"I will sprinkle clean water on you, and you will be clean; I will cleanse you from all your impurities and from all your idols. I will give you a new heart and put a new spirit in you; I will remove from you your heart of stone and give you a heart of flesh." (Ezekiel 36:25-26)

Through me, God has allowed my life to be a living testimony. Like Paul and Silas, God has turned my suffering into praise.

"About midnight Paul and Silas were praying and singing hymns to God, and the other prisoners were listening to them." (Acts 16:25)

Paul and Silas were arrested and brought before the magistrates for false allegations. They were beaten and thrown into prison. In their suffering, they were singing praise to God and giving thanks to Jesus! They filled the prison with the love of God and everyone heard their joy in a time of hardship.

Moments later God shook the very foundation of that prison. All the cell doors flew open and all the prisoners' chains came free. God showed His power to those who heard His servant's prayers and praise, so they might believe and be saved.

Paul and Silas reached not only other prisoners. They reached a jailer (a guard) who took them into his home. He found faith in Jesus Christ because of Paul and Silas. The jailer was saved and he and his family were baptized immediately.

"They replied, 'Believe in the Lord Jesus, and you will be saved-- you and your household.'" (Acts 16:31)

Paul and Silas were freed by the magistrates the next day. It is easy to say that their release was the miracle in this situation, but in my heart I believe the true miracle is how Paul and Silas helped other, even their jailer, during their suffering. Our pain should not be a reason to look the other way.

In our time of distress we all must reach out to help others that are in need. We must lift one another up and share what God has done in our lives, our heart, and spirit. I found Jesus in my time of need and He freed me from the path of distraction and self-hate. God rescued me from the lion's mouth.

"Be self-controlled and alert. Your enemy the devil prowls around like a roaring lion looking for someone to devour. Resist him, standing firm in the faith, because you know that your brothers throughout the world are undergoing the same kind of sufferings." (1 Peter 5:8-9)

My trial is drawing near but my freedom from prison is not the message of my testimony. Like Paul and Silas, my message is that through hardships, God is there to transform our lives. He is a God of love and forgiveness willing to work so many ways in your life. He set me free from a sentence for greater than what this world can do. He has blessed my life and He will do the same for you. He is faithful.

"Jesus answered, 'I am the way and the truth and the life. No one comes to the Father except through me.'" (John 14:6) "Then you will know the truth, and the truth will set you free." (John 8:32)

In all my Christian love, may God bless you in your struggles and be with you always. May grace and peace be upon you forever and ever. "The LORD bless you and keep you; the LORD make his face shine upon you and be gracious to you; the LORD turn his face toward you and give you peace." (Numbers 6:24-26)

Part Three:
Email Conversations on Callings
by Yong Hui McDonald and Grace Lee

Introduction

In November 2015, I gave a presentation about my personal prayer life at the Pastors' Prayer Retreat in Vancouver, Canada. I also brought Korean books, *Journey With Jesus, books 1-4,* and Transformation Project Prison Ministry (TPPM) brochures to share with people who came. After my presentation I met Grace Lee, a Korean woman.

She was not a pastor but she came along with others who attended this retreat. She shared how she had experience healing as she listened to how I prayed for my alcoholic and abusive father so he can quit drinking. I was persistent and prayed and prayed, thinking if I prayed hard enough, God would change my father and make him quit drinking.

My father had no intention to stop drinking. The Lord knew it and shared it with me. This understanding actually gave me peace. I accepted it, and I stopped praying for my father's drinking problem. What the Lord spoke to me came true. My father was drunk when he committed suicide.

The focus of the presentation was that sometimes God will say yes and sometimes no. We need to take the time to listen and hear God's voice and understand what we should do. I also shared how God helped me to forgive my father.

Grace had a father who was abusive and she had a difficult time forgiving him. She finally came to the conclusion that she had to forgive her father to find peace. She wanted to volunteer for TPPM and told me that she would translate English books to Korean. I planned to ask her to translate one of the inmates books, *Maximum Saints*, and the Lord told me to give her *Women Who Lead* to translate so that's what I did.

Since we met, Grace and I have been communicating via email. From the beginning, the Lord told me to use our email conversations in the book *Callings* but I didn't share this with Grace until the Lord asked me to share it. The Lord was leading Grace to respond to her calling through three different events.

The first event was visiting Colorado. The Lord told me that He had given her "a heart of a missionary" and asked me to invite her to Colorado to visit Adams County Detention Facility (ACDF) where I minister as a chaplain. In January 2016, Grace visited ACDF and attended a Transformation Project Prison Ministry (TPPM) celebration gathering. TPPM volunteers celebrated what God was doing to help prisoners and homeless in January 2016. Grace went back to Canada and started Praying Mothers Prison Ministry (PMPM) under TPPM and organized a group of women who gather together, pray for prisoners, and fundraise.

The Lord guided Grace to be involved in ministry by taking an initiative and organizing a group of people for prison ministry. She had a gift of leadership and started using it more to help prisoners. This might not have happened if she didn't visit Colorado. The Holy Spirit was leading her ministry path.

The second event was through translation. God shared a message with Grace through the book *Women Who Lead*. This book brought her healing while she was translating. This book was published in September 2016, which will help many others to learn about how God shapes and lead broken people into leadership. Translating and writing was a gift of hers. She did a great job.

The third event was how God was leading her ministry through school preparation. In September 2016, Grace started attending Seminary to pursue a Master of Divinity in order to serve God better in the future.

I am grateful that Grace helped in the preparation of this email conversations. I thank God that He is in control and leading this book.

Email Conversations On Callings

12/14/15

YH: Hi, Grace, you did a great job editing my first Korean story. I need help with Korean stories. Yes, the Lord will open the doors for you. I received an invitation to go to LA in January 2016, San Francisco in February, and possibly New Jersey in March. The Lord told me He will open more doors and asked me to get ready. So, try to listen to words from the Lord. He will guide you. Thanks for your prayers. I pray that the Lord will bless you beyond your imagination.

12/17/15

Grace: Thank you for your encouragement. This morning the Holy Spirit gently touched my heart with a scripture verse - Psalm 37:5. "Commit your way to the Lord, trust also in Him and He will do this." I am pondering how to commit my way to the Lord. It is still a bit unclear to me. I am so glad to hear that the Lord will enlarge the TPPM ministry. People who commit themselves to it are enormously blessed. I think it is a secret of His work - always greatly rewarding. Again, thank you for your prayers.

12/18/15

YH: "I am pondering how to commit my way to the Lord." To me this is telling us to get to know God's heart so we can do what God wants us to do. Again, it's going back to listening. Without listening, we can't understand His heart. I was going to ask for an extension for one year so I would have more time to finish my schooling. I need more time to do other things besides writing my dissertation and the Lord told me to finish it so I will graduate in 2016 instead of 2017.

He has other plans for me. I am trying to finish my dissertation next year. As long as I try to obey the voice of God, things will work out much better because He knows everything, and I don't. Do you have any daily devotional readings? If not, you might try *Loving God, 100 Daily Meditations and Prayer*. I am using *Loving God 3*, and it helps me to focus on God.

Grace: Hi Pastor McDonald, I just started reading *Loving God Volume 2*. I am so glad that I have this opportunity. I have a deep desire to love Him, but it wasn't easy. I will be a woman who loves the Lord more than before by the time I finish the book.

12/20/15

YH: I will be working on the book *Repentance*. It is one of the books the Lord asked me to write. Many inmates have asked me how to repent, and the book will give them some guidelines. All we have to do is ask God to forgive all the things we remember that we did that fell short of God's standard, and then ask the Holy Spirit to help us repent. It seems that people needed to be reminded of this. I actually didn't know it until I took repentance seriously in 2010.

The whole year my focus was asking the Holy Spirit to purify my soul through repentance. This opened a new door for repentance. God helped me to remember the things that I couldn't before. Anyway, repentance is the key for getting closer to the Lord. God knows the depth of our hearts and what needs to be cleansed. We can sometimes see the sin we justify but we can't see other things until the Holy Spirit reveals them to us. I believe that's why the Lord asked me to write a book on repenting.

Grace: Repentance, I think is what I need the most in my situation, but it is not obtained by my will or ability. I pray that the Lord plants a hatred of sin and a fear of the Lord in my heart on top of the spirit of repentance. Walking my journey with the Lord is fascinating so I am joyful and excited to do the work.

However, looking for a job is discouraging and stressful for me. It's already been over a month, and I feel like it distracts me from my faith. These days, I am not sure it is the Lord's will for me even though most of the women around me are working outside of their home and earning money. I think I have stress comparing others' lives to mine and I feel sheltered as a housewife. I've been praying that the Lord's will be done in my life.

12/21/15

YH: I've been praying for the Lord's will to be done in your life. The Lord will lead you to find a job if that's His will. You are praying. The Lord knows what you need and I pray that the Lord will guide you to be in a place where you need to work. What we really need is a close relationship with the Lord. If you keep spending more time with the Lord in silence and listening, He will share what He wants you to do.

Grace: Since I started the job search program, I often lose my priorities. Tonight, I will pray and meditate on His word. I applied for an ESL instructor position recently, but have not heard anything yet. I'd love to belong to the society and contribute something to the new immigrants. We will see. Waiting is not easy for me; I'll try to focus on worshiping the Lord and praying.

12/22/15

YH: The most important things the Lord told me to do so that I am able to teach others are: First, love God and second, listen to His voice. That's the reason God asked me to write the books *Loving God* and *Four Voices* to help recognize God's voice. *Loving God* is the most critical one and it requires daily discipline. God also directed me to write the *Loving God* book series. These books have mostly Scripture. Scripture brings God's presence to our spiritual life. That's why I use the *Loving God* books in my devotions. Yesterday's devotion was proclaiming victory in every situation in the name of the Lord.

Grace: Pastor McDonald, my group of ladies prayed for TPPM last Wednesday. The Vancouver area is quite passive spiritually, but we're hoping prayer can change the atmosphere. I didn't get any phone calls for a job interview. My husband is quite responsible and we can survive on one income, but I want to do something outside of the home and be financially independent.

Tomorrow, I will apply for another position – there is an opening for a library assistant. Anyhow, I would like to stop looking for a job for a while and plan for the new year and reduce distractions.

12/29/15
YH: I am glad that you are reading the Word more and trying to focus on the Lord. He will bless you for it. The Lord will open the door for you to find a job. Have you ever thought about pursuing some kind of ministry work as you are looking, something like a hospital chaplain or something of that nature? First you need to understand your calling, but your fulfillment in working comes when you serve God. Keep praying and the Lord will make things clear to you.

When I understood that my calling was ministry, I went to the seminary. Going to school was the only way I could prepare to serve God. Not only working as a prison chaplain but also a hospital chaplain. I can also work in a church as a pastor if I want to. My denomination has many mission work opportunities all over the world if I choose to work as a missionary. They even sponsor them.

The United Methodist Church gives minority female pastors many opportunities to serve in different capacities. Consequently, while I was ministering to prisoners I received the largest scholarships from my denomination and my school when I went to seminary. I am called to work with prisoners and I am very happy with that. When you can, come to visit Colorado for a couple of days. You can visit my ministry setting and try to listen to God. Pray about it and let me know if God asks you to visit Colorado.

"Those who seek me earnestly will find me."
These are the words that the Lord gave me when I first seriously tried to spend time in prayer and this is what I feel God is asking me to give you. Have a blessed day.

Grace: I've been looking for a position where I can provide help and care for others, so I couldn't apply just anywhere. Customer service at Safeway is a place where I can help others, but I am looking for a deeper level of helping - seeing people become the person whom God wants her or him to be. This afternoon, I asked myself, "Is working as a library assistant really what I want to do in life?" While I was preparing my resume and cover letter I answered myself, "No."

Right off the bat, I checked my email to take a break, and was surprised. I felt like someone knows about me deeply and thoroughly as I read your email. My deepest desire is serving Him and His people rather than just working and earning money.

Thank you so much for your offer. I'd like to visit you, but I want my husband to support me as a sign of agreement. I will pray about it. Writing emails and praying for me are such thoughtful gifts for me. It is priceless. Would you be accountable for me in 2016?

I want to spend 2016 in prayer and dedicate myself to His word. I have had this thought for decades, but never practiced it successfully. I tried it alone over and over, but every time I faced distractions and failed. I planned to attend a Culinary Program in April and study there until October 2016. However, it could be a distraction during the year even though it sounds good to me.

I stopped going to the Job Finding Program because I have a strong sense that the Lord hired me. I don't expect anything big in the worldly view, but I want to walk the path He has prepared for me. I am joyful because the Lord is my employer; I have the best boss on earth! My job next year is prayer and meditating on God's word. And I believe He will give me some work continually – mainly volunteering for TPPM. Praise the Lord!

12/30/15

YH: I am very happy to know that you have a heart to serve God. I asked the Lord what I should focus on in 2016. In 2010 my prayer focus was on repenting and the other years, I sort of changed my prayer focus throughout the year. But this time I want to stay focused because the Lord told me that I shouldn't extend my dissertation paper one more year because He had something else for me the following year. Therefore, I plan to pursue, finish it and graduate in May 2016.

The Lord gave me the topic for my prayer focus in 2016 the other day. I asked Him if He had anything to say, He said, "I will lead you. I will teach you how to love me." This is going to be my prayer focus in 2016. Praise God! My ministry loves others but loving God has to be first. He taught me that I fell into the trap of loving ministry more than God and it causes me to neglect spending time with Him in prayer and daily devotion. If I don't listen to His heart, I will fall into a trap of loving something more than God. Even loving ministry more than God is not acceptable to Him.

Even when I try to do well, I can fall into the trap of pleasing myself and others more than God. That's why

I am glad that God called me to silent prayer to listen and wait on Him. It's so easy to fall into the trap of following our own plans. I have seen people trying to just focus on making money instead of waiting on God to understand what God wants them to do. Then they end up wasting money and time on things they don't need.

People who have the heart to please God and serve Him, shouldn't focus on making money first. The first priority is to find out what God wants. In your case, it is the same. If you follow your own plans, you will end up regretting it. So, I can tell you what the Lord told me after He asked me to offer you the opportunity to come to Colorado for a visit to listen to God. I asked the Lord, "Why do you want me to invite her to Colorado?" He answered, "I called her to be in missionary. I gave her the heart of a missionary." Now, I am in a foreign country and working with many nationalities so I am a missionary and if you teach English for many nationalities, you will also be a missionary.

Being allowed to teach Christ versus teaching others technical learning, such as English, are totally different. You will get paid to share your own knowledge and skill by teaching English. Sharing God and His plans for others is sharing what God offers. There is a big difference. It depends on their calling. If someone is called to be an administrator in mission work, they will be happy teaching technical things. But that's not my calling. My calling is to share Christ with others. That gives me the most satisfaction in my life. I can't be happy with any other vocation because ministry is my calling.

For example, after I graduated from Iliff School of Theology, I was waiting to find ministry work and was able to work as a part time, on-call hospital chaplain and as a medical interpreter. I felt my life was wasted because my deep desire and yearning was to share Christ with others. Where did this come from? God made me this way. I didn't realize it for a long time until I finally started paying attention to God's voice in my heart.

The Lord has given me the desire to serve God in a full capacity, not in a part-time or other helping position. Being a medical interpreter paid my bills but left me with dissatisfaction. That was not what I was called to do or made to do. So, I am very happy that the Lord helped me to pursue ministry - which gave me more satisfaction than any other job I had before, including computer work that I loved.

I was born to be a minister. This is the conclusion I finally had. This understanding gave me such joy and I am glad that my 3-years of study prepared me to be a full-time minister. Without the education, I couldn't be where I am today. I am able to use my ministry skill to help others. I am amazed by how I get paid to pray with others, preach, and lead worship. These are things that I love because I see the Holy Spirit's blessing on others and God's leading hands in my ministry with book projects. I couldn't be happier! I would be happy even if I died tomorrow. I have followed my calling to serve God to the fullest.

Pursing my Doctor of Ministry wasn't my idea. I didn't need any more education. The Lord asked me to do it and I received a full scholarship. The school paid for everything including my books, residence program expenses, as well as a trip overseas. This is also God's gift and He told me He was answering my prayers that "Lord, use me to the maximum for your glory." Many people see education as a qualification to teach and lead.

I was called to train leaders from the beginning of my ministry. I have led many pastors' retreats and spoken to them about prison ministry. In order for God to use me to the fullest, He has to train me to be a leader in the human sense - which included going through the ordination process and also obtaining the necessary education.

I pray that the Lord will make things clear to you. I have many who learned to listen to the Lord's voice and they are now able to discern what God wants them to do. Your daily devotional life and illumination of distraction in life can help you listen to God and He will help you sort out what you should do with your vocation. Understanding your calling can be one of your prayer focuses. This comes with "Those who seek me earnestly will find me." Seek God's direction patiently. Listening in silence will help Him to share His heart.

When I decided to go through the ordained ministry process, there was a way to become a local pastor without going through seminary. I could have attended one month of ministry training and worked in a church as a pastor. What God wanted from me was 100% commitment to serve Him. So, I told my husband I would finish my Master of Divinity just like he did and be available to serve God to the fullest.

I was right. The chaplaincy I applied for required ordination and also a Master of Divinity to even interview for the position. I am glad that I listened to the Lord and not my husband. He was selfish and wanted to just have me by his side to support his ministry. He didn't realize that I had a calling to respond to. I had to forgive him for that. Each individual's calling is different but the Holy Spirit can reveal what God really wants. Until then, we have to wait and sort out what He wants us to do.

I am glad that you are sorting everything out with God's help. He will make everything clear to you as you wait. In your spare time, why don't you start writing your journey of "Forgiveness" and "Healing." While you reflect, the Lord can bring you healing in areas you need. You will also learn to listen to God as you reflect and wait for Him. I know you are busy, but this practice might clear your mind. Many peoples' minds are so full of so many events in life that they don't know how to purify their thoughts so they can't listen to God's voice.

1/2/16

Grace: Pastor McDonald, first of all, wishing you a happy and a blessed new year! Thank you for the email; there is so much stuff I need to ponder and this is solid food for me. In your writing, "I was born to be a minister... I can't be happier..." I can hardly even imagine that kind of conviction.

Since I experienced being born-again when I was 15 years old, I have strived to achieve various things based on social conventions - getting married, raising two children, pursuing growth in a multi-cultural community, and looking for a good career, but I have never experienced true contentment. Living by the world's standards never gave me that.

In the evening I had a vision; I saw an elephant that was released from a cage, but didn't know what happened to her and she was completely ignorant about what she could do with her new found freedom and privilege, so she just sat on the ground. However, Jesus was there with her and offered His hand to hold. The elephant intuitively sensed that He would lead and guide her to a new life. Pastor McDonald, I think the elephant was me. I'd like to visit you and the Adams County Detention Facility; I will keep on praying about it this month. I will also pray for your essay.

YH: This is a great beginning in listening to God. When God starts communicating with you in a vision like that He will speak to you more and more. There is a woman who supports TPPM. She first didn't hear God's voice but she noticed that in every prayer project, I asked people to read the Gospels to get to know Jesus. She did that to learn about Jesus and practiced listening in silence, and the Lord started speaking to her heart. The key to listening is to get to know Jesus' heart. Start asking him questions and He will be happy to answer you.
Three things that I learned from the Lord are:
1. God can speak to people in their heart. I thought God would only speak to us with an audible voice like people do. Also, I thought God only speaks to prophets and special people in the Bible. The Lord taught me how to listen by making me wait in silence. Then He told me to teach others how to listen. I taught people to listen and those who followed the instructions were able to listen to God and their relationship with God changed for the better.
2. Jesus wants to walk with us, share his heart of love and teach us that learning to love God is more important than serving. People can't serve God with passion if they don't understand Jesus' heart for the lost souls. So, listening to JESUS' HEART is what we should focus on. Talking to Jesus as the most loving and intimate person in the world is the door to understanding

our calling. The calling we have in Christ is the most fulfilling road that we can ever find. Praise God! I am blessed to know that Jesus is leading my path. If I had known what a glorious walk this was, I would have gone into the ministry earlier. I wasted many years of resisting my calling and I am glad that God didn't give up on me, for it's by His grace that I am in the ministry.

3. I didn't know the power of the Holy Spirit. The Holy Spirit guided me to pray, read the Gospels, and listen to God. Then as I got to know more about Jesus, I got to know more about the Holy Spirit's leading in my life. The Holy Spirit started giving me assignments by speaking to my heart with or without words, and through understanding and convictions. As I started obeying the Holy Spirit, I started to grow into a trusting and loving relationship with Jesus.

Grace: Hired by Him – I am His prayer agent who represents Jesus and a friend of the suffering. "Thank you, Lord, I am so glad that I am hired by you; I am willing to be a faithful servant of you. Whenever You show me your people who need prayers, I will do it gladly because it is the God-given career for my life. Jesus, I am so excited to have that position. In addition, I will feed your lambs because I love you."

Hi Pastor McDonald, the reason I started writing a short journal was to remove distractions in my journey this year. I really want to be preoccupied with Him and hope it will be my lifestyle for the rest of my life. Accepting the calling is like a Google Map; I feel like I am not in the wilderness anymore. I wished to be a devoted servant of Him, but I wasn't sure that He chose me as His full-time servant. However, I know now that I am destined to be a fisher of men. Having the correct identity makes a difference in my daily life and it already gives me fulfillment.

1/3/16

YH: Great! That's how I start the day, with devotion and listening to God through Scripture and prayer and listening to His voice. God has given you mission work through prayer and caring for others.

1/21/16

Grace: I finished reading *Journey With Jesus*. It is one of the best gifts from the Lord in my life, and reading it once is not enough. I will read it again. Last week, I was a bit depressed. Sometimes, I try to talk about it to people around me, but I receive the same responses most of the time: "You don't know how fortunate you are. Your husband is working hard for his family and faithful to you. What else do you need? You don't know reality and you need to grow." Sounds all right, but from time to time, I feel life is meaningless.

While I was reading *Journey With Jesus*, I was surprised and amazed by the Lord Jesus; how much He longs for having relationship with us! It is beyond my imagination. He told me, "Grace, I want you to have a deeper relationship with me. You carry many burdens alone and you ignore me most of the time. I have been waiting for you to pay attention to me and openly share your heart. I know you believe in me, but I want you to know me more and appreciate me."

For a few days, I couldn't say much; I am still thinking about what I can say to Jesus. Even though I have been a faithful and hardworking believer, what the

Lord said to me is so right. I've been staying at my comfort zone, and I didn't treat Him as a person. However, the Lord showed me through that book that a relationship with him is more important than anything else.

While I was reading the book, I felt Jesus was with me; I was thrilled that He and I have something in common - a desire for a relationship. Yesterday, I tried to pray silently and listen to His voice after lunch, but was sleepy in a few minutes. I had a cup of tea but was sleepy again. I took a nap and then another cup of tea. I tried and tried, but didn't hear anything. I ate an apple and couldn't help bursting into laughter. Listening to His voice through silent prayer was comical and hilarious.

However, Jesus said to me in the evening, "Grace, you can claim a conversation with me because you are my bride and I am your groom." I felt very close to Him. I have been preoccupied with knowing Jesus and pondering about Him. The Lord will lead me somewhere I've never been. Thank you for your obedience of writing *Journey with Jesus*. The book has blessed me immensely.

YH: God will speak when He wants but as you develop an intimate relationship with Him, you will hear Him more often. He also makes us wait at times. I even thought about divorcing my husband one time when he didn't support my decision to go into the ministry. God changed my heart by saying my husband helped me the most in my preparation for my ministry. Listening to God's voice saved our marriage.

We expect too much from other human beings. When we are filled with God's love because of our intimate relationship with God, we no longer focus on receiving love from people but have overflowing love, compassion, and understanding for others. That's when our focus is sharing God's love but most of all, we can forgive.

I learned that we can't be completely satisfied in a relationship even if we try. We are all faulty and weak human beings. The reason for that is we are creatures who are made to have a complete loving relationship with God first. When "loving God with a passion" develops in our hearts, we will have more understanding of what we can do to build a close relationship with others. Even so, we may or sometimes we may not have a closer relationship with other people. It depends on how they walk with the Lord. We can be closer to people who walk closely with Him. That's why we have to let go of our expectations of searching for love in people and pursue our relationship with Jesus.

When our hearts are filled with Jesus' love, our focus changes according to what the Lord wants. That's when we can be a better spouse for our marriage partner. *Journey With Jesus Two* tells that in detail. When you have the heart of God, your desires and focus is not the same because He wants you to walk with Him to get to know Him. To do that we have to let go of what we may treasure which are our own plans and desires that we focus on and want to have. We hold and treasure many things but the Lord wants all of us to change our focus to His heart. He wants our pure desire to be to follow Him. I believe you are on the right path.

One more thing about how God makes us wait is in the book of Exodus 24:12-18. God spoke to Moses many times Moses didn't have to wait but had answers right away. Even after God called Moses to come up to the mountain, He made Moses wait for 6 days on the mountain then the 7th day, the Lord spoke to Moses. God makes us wait at times. What's important is that we are paying attention to God. He knows that we are ready to listen to Him. This is the email I received from Mike: "Have you considered having a movie, or even a play, made from your *Journey With Jesus* books? Seems all we'd have to do is get it in the hands of a Christian filmmaker, and they would run with it. Mike."

1/22/16

Grace: It is not a coincidence. I also thought about that *Journey With Jesus* should be a movie. Now, my mom has been reading the book. The book is His, and He must have a great plan for it. It will have an impact on many people and bring a breakthrough. I pray that many believers dedicate their lives to the Lord for the Great Harvest through the book and the movie in the future.

Many of us are still stuck in the religious realm, but *Journey With Jesus* connects us to the Lover of our souls. So many times, *Journey With Jesus* reminded me of Song of Songs while I was reading. The depth of Song of Songs is still a mystery to me, but *Journey With Jesus* vividly reveals the relationship between the Lover and beloved in modern time language and setting. In addition, the main character will be a girl, so the movie will be for all ages and families. It will be magnificent. Praise the Lord; He wants to continually give us a gift. His gift is always purposeful and life changing.

YH: I pray that the Lord will use His story to the maximum. I always thought an animated movie would be good and could help others but I didn't think about a movie with actors. When I went to a prayer school in Canada, Reverend Park's wife told me that a movie would be good if JWJ was made into an animated movie. I never told her my thoughts. So, if God wants it to, it could be made into both. I thought if Mel Gibson takes this project, it could be done well but I don't know how to go about it. I believe the Lord will lead us to the right people.

1/24/16

Grace: It was such a hectic week. On top of that, I attended a Christian conference in my neighbor this weekend. It was good, but I am not sure that it was beneficial for me. Well, next time, I will ask the Lord if I should attend that kind of event or not. I lost track of the whole week. There are so many Christian activities, but spending time with the Lord gives me the best, first hand, and life-changing experiences.

I have been reading Matthew these days. I was deeply touched by 13:44-45. The Lord Jesus is a Treasure hidden in a field. I have been receiving His blessings all the time, but never seriously thought about giving up myself to find the Treasure.

Frankly, I am far from self-denial. I've collected Chinaware, accessories, Christmas ornaments, nice clothing…I've prayed to have a puppy and dreamed about a romantic relationship. Well, I am not a person who sells everything to buy fine Pearls. However, verses 45-46 say, "The kingdom of heaven is like a merchant looking for fine pearls. When he found one of great value…" Knowing His worthiness should come first and that is my prayer these days. Both keeping what I have and obtaining the Pearl would be my wish. It took a long time to consider buying the treasure because my life was worldly and carnal, 'half-hearted.'

By the way, my husband is a devoted father, and he cares about our daughter dearly. I am grateful for that. Once in a while, I ask our daughter how she feels about having a loving father. She says, "I don't know how I feel about it, mom, but I know how much he cares for me."

In fact, she takes counseling at school and anti-depressant due to sleeping and anxiety disorders. I feel like she has to have a perfect life, but she has many issues.

You are right, Pastor McDonald; we have a certain empty space that is impossible to fill without God. The solution is our Lord Jesus. This year, I will try to be whole-hearted to the Lord and He will reveal Himself to me.

1/25/16

YH: It's great that you have a loving and caring husband. As I hear it, your daughter needs healing from the Lord. If she seeks God like you do and focuses on God she will find peace and healing in her heart. My book, *Tornadoes of Spiritual Warfare,* talks about healing from different spirits. The spirit of fear is one that can bring anxiety. I think your daughter may be hearing many negative voices in her mind. The *Four Voices* also describes how people suffer from the wrong voices. She needs someone who can understand her spiritual condition. I pray that she will encounter Jesus to find peace and healing.

Anyway, I am so glad that the Lord is helping you to see your spiritual condition and you are on the road to know him at a deeper level. Praise God. Also, when you truly find peace with God and learn to listen to Him, you can help your daughter from a spiritual level that your daughter desperately needs.

1/26/16

Grace: Mat. 16:12b "...But against the teaching of the Pharisees and Sadducees." Hundreds people attended the Conference that I attended last weekend. It was two days conference, but the entire teaching was only three hours and Jesus was not the main idea. I found that we believers often ignore whom we serve and who the director is. Since I tasted the richness of the relationship with Jesus Himself, I realized everything is in Him. I remember one of the verses somewhere in the Bible, "Knowing Him is doing His work." Having events and programs might be a trend among North American Christians. I hope the movement of listening to His voice will arise among us.

Thank you for the wake-up calls, Pastor McDonald! I read the Korean version of *Tornadoes of Spiritual Warfare* today in order to pray for my daughter. A few weeks ago, my son Derek told me, "Mom, the explanation in the book is effective and articulate." He had been struggling with spiritual warfare and nightmares. I think that many questions inside of him were answered while he read the book. He was released from the darkness, even though he didn't talk about it in detail with me. I also received a great deal of help; it was eye opening and gave me a deeper understanding of what is behind human behaviors.

Last Friday afternoon, I was discouraged because of my sister and didn't know how to recover, but now I know it was a spiritual attack. The main force that discourages me is the devil and it is using my sister's bitterness. I began to pray for her as well. Furthermore, I am ready to forgive her because it wasn't about her wickedness, but weakness. So much to say, but I am now hopeful for my daughter's future and the relationship between her and me. I will consistently pray for the spiritual battles in her until I see the results. Praise the Lord!

YH: I am glad that you can utilize the books. I give thanks to God that He has all the power to bring healing and releases us from all the things that entangle us. I am proud of you.

Grace: Dear Pastor McDonald, thank you for your prayer and the book *The Ultimate Parenting Guide*. I read it last night. I was deeply touched by the authenticity and comforted by the victory you experienced in the Lord. I tried to pray for my daughter this morning, but I was heavy-hearted because of a headache. Spontaneously, I fell asleep for three hours and tried it again after lunch, but became sleepy again. I took a nap for four hours. I was tired, but I went to bed early last night and slept enough. Therefore, it is not about physical. While I was praying for my daughter yesterday morning, I was struggling with feelings of tediousness, tiredness, and avoidance. Eventually, I fell asleep.

My daughter has been suffering from anxiety and a sleeping disorder for almost ten years. It was tough; I was suspicious about the spiritual warfare, but I lacked in knowledge. I didn't tenaciously pursue winning the battle. Now, she doesn't go to church anymore and is not around believers since she lives in the dorm at her university. I just assumed that she would be OK. I will stop avoiding the issues and kneel down to Him. In the meantime, I'd like to send a letter to her. I just would like to share what I wrote to her.

Hannah my dearest,

How are you doing? Eating well and sleeping well? You have been managing the issues well through counseling and stuff. However, I believe God's word is the best remedy for you.

My dear, what are you afraid of? Think about fear in your heart. Let's remove it through prayers and His Truth.

Psalms 32:8 "I will instruct you and teach you in the way you should go: I will counsel you and watch over you."

Every day, spend some time in His word. That is mama's wish for you. He is your Wonderful Counselor. Remember the relationship between the Lord Jesus and you. It is real like the relationship between you and me. It is not a religious doctrine. Jesus Himself is powerful and mighty. His truth is absolute, and He is on your side.

I love you madly.

Hugs,

Mama

My Dear girl,

Have you thought about how to forgive someone and ask forgiveness from the Lord?

I am not perfect, but it helped me get released from bondage and unhappiness. One at a time! Ask the

Lord Jesus whom you need to forgive.

This morning, I read Matthew 20:6b-7 "'Why have you been standing here all day long doing nothing?' 'Because no one has hired us,' they answered. He said to them, 'You also go and work in my vineyard.'"

Hannah, I'd like to surprise you. I have been hired by the Lord for His vineyard. I grinned because of His sense of humor while reading the verses. I felt like He had seen my situation and what I wanted.

As you know, I searched for work, but the result - being hired by Him was a total surprise. I don't have a job description yet, but He will lead me step by step. He will amaze you and me; I also wait for him expectantly. These days, He shows me His grace and mercy doubly; it happened right after I started obeying Him and stopped attending the Job Ready Program. I tried to get close to Him. I learned there is nothing to hold too tightly, but Jesus.

Anyhow, that is my journey with the Lord Jesus. Yours may be different from mine, but there is a principal "Obedience." You know how much I was thrilled to raise you because I knew He gave me His princess in my life. Always remember that you are not just His, but also His princess and His treasure. He adores you and admires you.

It's not cold anymore. I saw some of the buds on the trees in the backyard, and I no longer have black clouds in my mind. My thoughts are clear and every morning. It is new to me. You recommended me to take counseling and attend a support group because you thought that I was going through a mid-life crisis. Thankfully, the Lord Jesus Himself became my Wonderful Counselor and I've been basking in Him. Ask Him to be your Wonderful counselor, He will be.

I just miss you badly, and still remember you as a little girl painting butterflies, playing with candlelight, and eating barbecued marshmallows. To me, your chubby cheeks were the cutest things on earth. Have a great day!

So much love,

Mama

1/27/16

YH: You wrote two wonderful letters to your daughter. I am glad you are sharing them. I am glad that you are growing so you can make a difference in your daughter's life. You are trying to pull your daughter out of misery. When you try to pray and you have a difficult time, many times it is the devil attacking you so you can't pray for others.

God is the only answer in finding peace and healing. You are showing that to your daughter. Spiritual discernment is critical in spiritual warfare, but many don't know it. I believe you have that gift of discernment and you were feeling spiritual oppression. As you get closer to the Lord, you will be bothered less and less. I am proud of you. I pray for your daughter that the Lord will surround her with angels to protect her and bring healing in her spirit.

Grace: What encouragement! Thank you for your prayer and sending the book *Tornadoes of Spiritual Warfare.* It is a wonderful study guide. Visiting Adams

County Detention Facility was a significant experience for me. The Lord was the center of the trip, so it was inspirational. Being led by the Holy Spirit is interesting. I didn't see that you prepared for your worship services, but it was full. I was impressed by it. Martha worked hard to prepare for the meeting with Jesus, but Mary relaxed and focused on what He was saying. The Holy Spirit must have led the worship services there.

I facilitated a ladies meeting this afternoon and I spent time with the Lord in the morning reading the end of Matthew, trying to listen to His voice and praying. I didn't prepare for the ladies' meeting because I planned to be led by the Holy Spirit this time like the worship service at Adams County Detention Facility.

As soon as we started the meeting, Linda began to share some verses in Hebrews and James. We also shared our experiences and interpretations related to the verses and then I explained what I learned from the book *Four Voices*.

It was so good to let the Spirit move around us. I learned that I don't have to have any pressure for the meeting and depend on the formula.

Just spending time with Him and dwelling on His truth in my daily life is the key to inviting people to Jesus. It boils down to the verse Galatians 2:20 "I no longer live, but Christ lives in me." I tasted a glimpse of it, but it was beneficial for the group of ladies and me.

I want to continually learn about letting the Holy Spirit work through me. Many times, I was scared of crucifying myself because it felt like I would be losing all the pleasure and uniqueness of me. However, I've been learning these days that God can give me a deeper sense of pleasure.

People like Mother Teresa probably knew God given happiness even though she didn't have luxuries. She lived life more fully than others who are self-serving. God's pleasure is still a mystery to me and "Christ lives in me," is a complicated idea to me. He will teach me more because I have a desire to know Him.

Healing is always the sooner it happens better. If the students encounter the Lord when they are in the Youth Custody Services, they will not get into serious trouble down the road. I am thinking about starting a support group for the youth in prison. The support group means a group of mothers can pray and provides Christian books for the students in the facility.

The mothers will visit them regularly to get to know the students' needs and prayer requests. I believe most of the youth in the facility don't have mothers who fervently pray for them. Some of us can do it for them and it will make a difference in their future. I pray that the mothers get trained as intercessory prayer warriors and that the Lord will open the door for us.

While I was reading the book, *The Ultimate Parenting,* I was impressed by the relationship between you and your mother. You introduce your mother as a prayer warrior; her prayer and dedication to the Lord had a great impact on you and your ministry. It reminded me of my tough teenage years. I had to pray day in and day out by myself; otherwise I wouldn't survive in my abusive home environment; at the time, I wondered if there was anyone who could pray for me. However, the past is past; I can be that kind of mother now for the youth in the facility. In worldly perspectives, they are lacking in many areas, but mothers' prayer will cover it and "They shall not be in want." Psalm 23:1.

The day before yesterday, I named the organization, "Praying Mothers Prison Ministry." I tried to get some information today, but I found that is not easy. I need a lawyer. Can you establish a sister organization known as PMPM under TPPM? The reason I want to have the organization is to spread and share the idea to many people. In addition, PMPM can be supervised and nurtured by TPPM. If it is not suitable for being as an organization, that's fine.

Your visit to San Francisco is coming soon and then the next one is the United Methodist Women's Gathering in California. I will pray for your trip that the ladies will be inspired and compassionate for the people in prison.

2/5/16

YH: I am amazed by what God is doing. "Praying Mothers Prison Ministry" will please the Lord and I am happy to hear that the Lord is blessing you with visions to help prisoners. At this point, you don't need to find a lawyer, if TPPM can work with your vision to start a new ministry. Later, after you are involved in lots of fundraising for children like what Esther wants to do and you have potential donors for that specific purpose of funding prisoners' education, that's the time you want to start a new non-profit. Starting Praying Mothers and ministering to prisoners, you can work with TPPM since there is no other funding involved.

I will bring this up to the TPPM board for an approval so TPPM can work with PMPM. We can be a big family working for the Lord and for the prisoners. Before I bring it to the board, I would like to make following suggestions.

1. Start organizing people anyway - and contact the local youth center and start the ministry with other ladies under the name of PMPM. In this way, you don't have to wait for TPPM. I believe this vision that you have is from the Lord. Start organizing and figuring out how you can spread this ministry.

2. Work on a mission statement and the application for this ministry for mothers who may be interested in it. I will send you a copy of the Peace Officers Peace Project (POPP) application, so you just have to adopt it.

3. You should be the coordinator of PMPM, so TPPM can work with you. This ministry can grow as it is formed, distributing books, teaching, mentoring, and praying for the youth.

4. Start thinking about a brochure so you can start recruiting people for PMPM. Working with TPPM will be perfect since we just adopted a new mission statement that we will be working with leaders in the community and in prisons. I am attaching a TPPM updated by-law for you. Here is a part of TPPM mission statement:

> Transformation Project Prison Ministry (TPPM) brings hope and encouragement. It offers healing to the incarcerated, disadvantaged, and to people affected by incarceration, by publishing and distributing books and media free of charge. TPPM also facilitates the development of Christian leaders who speak inside and outside of prisons, and in churches and at community events to spread the good news of the Gospel message of Jesus Christ.

God bless you and your ministry of PMPM. What a great idea to start a ministry with praying. He will bless you through this. Keep organizing PMPM as the Lord leads you. I love your vision for praying, reaching out with books, and mentoring youth.

3/4/16

Grace: I am grateful for the double portion of blessings from the Lord. Yesterday, I sent some books to the chaplains of the Youth Custody Centers in my province, BC. We've been praying for the chaplains in the Youth Custody Center to be revived and be filled with the Holy Spirit to minister the youngsters. Our next step is to send books to the chaplains at the regular adult prisons in BC with prayers. Even though we are not sending the books to the inmates yet, we are glad that we at least sent the books to chaplains, have been praying for them, and their ministries.

5/29/16

Grace: I have had the same dream at night on a regular basis. There is a test, and I always fail it. However, the test wasn't that hard, but I didn't know where I needed to put my answers. I didn't have enough marks in total and failed. The dream is annoying. It is so real and I freaked out in my dream.

Recently, I thought about getting in the Culinary Program. It's free because it is a government supported program for certain people who don't have a job. However, my husband is surprisingly positive and supportive about my schooling. He said that I'd better take the seminary course (Master of Divinity) as soon as possible and he will pay the entire school fee.

YH: This is great news! Praise God that your husband is supportive of your study. God will lead you if you try to serve Him. I am sure you are asking the Lord already about the dream and keep asking Him what your dream means. He will reveal it to you. I am trying to learn how to make a book cover now so I will be focusing on that and that will help TPPM in the long run and save cover costs.

Grace: I've never dreamed the same kind of dream continually; it troubles me because I don't want to fail the test. I will keep on asking God how I can pass the test.

5/31/16
Grace: Thank you for your prayer. Last night I laughed for a while. Why can't God tell me straightforwardly? Why does He tell me through dreams? He is funny. I know He wanted to get my attention. I dropped the Culinary Program today and began to translate the book, *Women Who Lead*. My decision is based on my relationship with Jesus. I think I still don't know the whole meaning of the dream, but I will keep on asking Him.

YH: Hi, Grace, you said, "I dropped the Culinary Program today and began to translate *Women Who Lead*." Praise God! Sometimes we don't have the luxury of choosing how we spend our time. That's why I had to obey the Lord and finish my school. I am glad I did. I see the culinary school as a luxury for some people. I am sure you were listening to God and made a good decision. I am so glad that you are translating *Women Who Lead*. I trust that you will do a great job with the translation. As you translate, I believe the Lord will speak to you as well.

Grace: I am so glad that you agree with my decision. Lately, I don't get agitated but I am just focused. I have more peace with the Lord. The after-effect of obeying God is huge. Thankfully, the Lord removed the strong desire of the Culinary Program from my heart. I've been enjoying translating. It's so fulfilling to me. This Friday morning, I will meet one of the academic advisers at the seminary to discuss the coursework starting this September. I pray the book *Women Who Lead* will encourage many Korean women down the road.

6/1/16
YH: Time is precious and we have no time to waste. I am so glad that you are going forward with theological education. Yes, I believe the Mennonite Program will be a good one. They have a very good reputation. Theological education is quite important in ministry not to mention your credibility as a spiritual leader. It also will give you more understanding and Biblical knowledge and what others are doing to enhance the Kingdom of God. I believe your translation will help many other women and men.

Grace: Thank you for your encouragement! Actually, people around me, specifically church people, are discouraging me about my further education, but it has been one of my deepest desires for long time. I am glad that my husband and you are supportive to me. I will keep on trying to follow the Holy Spirit.

YH: I am so glad that you are focusing on serving the Lord. It's great that your husband is encouraging you to study. The Lord will help you. I've experienced a few disappointments these days.

Grace: The Lord brought me closer to Him again and purified me through difficult times. I've been meditating on Joshua 1:9 "Be strong and courageous. Do not be terrified; do not be discouraged, for the Lord your God will be with you wherever you go." I will let you know how it goes.

YH: I am glad that you are working on a journey of studying and preparing to serve God.

6/7/16
Grace: Thank you Pastor McDonald, studying is my desire, but I am not sure that will prepare me for God's work. I hope and pray it will be. This morning, I attended an intense summer class as a trial from 8:30am to 12:30pm at the seminary. I was fascinated with being there. Surprisingly, it was interesting. I was confused many times during the lecture. Their academic words were like a foreign language to me. Theological terms will be challenging to me not only when listening but also when I write.
I still can't believe that I am almost there. It was one of my deepest desires for decades, but I suppressed it over and over again because I couldn't see it as a practical tool for my future. It was such a great day for me. Thank you for your prayers!

YH: I think it's great that you will be studying in

English even though some of the terms may be difficult and foreign to you. It will all come together as time goes by. Many Americans struggle as well. I worked very hard and it was worth it. We are limited on what we can do when we try to serve God without proper training in theology.

We may feel ready but others wouldn't recognize that you are. There are many others who can speak English better than me and they can preach better than me. They don't have a Master of Divinity, so others think they are not qualified to be a chaplain. They can't even get an interview without a degree.

In the long run, study is worthwhile because it is taught by others who are serving God and have devoted their lives to teach the Bible.

You are so far ahead. Many other foreign students struggle with English but you don't. I always had to have someone edit my papers even as I finished my dissertation. Actually, that helped me to be humble. English is my weakness and I can't even write in Korean well but the Lord uses me regardless. So, don't be discouraged or intimidated by study or the many new terms. I am sure the Lord will help you in your endeavor.

Grace: It is such a blessing to have someone ahead of me. I will go for it as long as the Lord opens the door for me. I can't live the way I have been anymore. I want to go further. The director sent me an email this evening. It is about their entirely new program coming out this semester, Chaplaincy Certificate Program. It is for people who completed their master degree. I planned to take the Master of

Arts in Christian Studies, which is a basic master course at the seminary. In the future, I will consider taking the Chaplaincy Certificate Program as well as the extended study, Master of Divinity. By the way, I didn't have the same dream last week. I am laughing again. I know He is not nasty, absolutely not, but mischievous. Good night!

6/8/16

YH: I strongly encourage you to take Master of Divinity if you can. I'll tell you why you should do this. All the other degree courses can be good enough for some part-time ministers, but you can't be considered or accepted as a spiritual leader, pastor or chaplain here in the U.S. without the Master of Divinity.

I don't know about Canada but there are different expectations in different spiritual leaderships. I can give you one example. One Korean woman came to Iliff School of Theology after she felt called to the ministry. She didn't want to be a local church pastor so she took the Master of Theological study. It was a two-year program.

After graduation, she worked in a social service department without being able to use her degree. Without the Master of Divinity, she couldn't work in full-time ministry. She finally figured out that her calling isn't just working in the social work but full-time ministry. Eventually, she had to go back to school and finish her Master of Divinity. She had to go through two more years to finish it because they had different course requirements. Master of Divinity is three years program. She now is working full-time in ministry. She also works part time as a hospital chaplain. I told her about the hospital part time chaplaincy.

I believe your call is ministry so if you work on a Master of Divinity and start working on an ordination process, that will lead you on the right track of going farther with ministry. If you can work with a denomination where they can open the door for ministry. I recommend a United Methodist denomination if you can because they have many ministry opportunities – missionary or church work or mission agencies. You can be a chaplain if you like which I am now and it's a big denomination to work with many people.

That's one of the reasons TPPM is growing, because in the U.S., Korean United Methodist Women are very active in missions and they accepted TPPM as one of their mission projects. You will be much happier if you are in full-time ministry because God has given you the heart for ministry. The only reason I went to seminary for my Master of Divinity was so that God would open the door for ministry. I worked with United Methodists because my husband was a United Methodist minister. It worked out well for me. United Methodists recognize and values women's ministry and they have many programs to help ethnic minorities with scholarships. I had more privileges as an ethnic woman. If you were actually a member of the United Methodist church and going through the ordination process, you could apply for many different scholarships. That's why I had a full scholarship.

My thought is that I don't need to work with any church or denomination where women or minority women in spiritual leadership are not valued or accepted. Time is short. I don't have time to debate with people who limit my ministry in anyway. You can pray about what's best for you. The Lord will lead you.

Grace: I think people freak out more when I show my interest in the Master of Divinity course. Anyhow, I am about to start online application for the Master of Divinity program. My motive is simple; I want to be fully equipped and available for the Lord, and whatever He asks me to do. However, it doesn't appeal to people around me; they are baffled. Seeing their astonishment is also hilarious to me. I don't know why God does something to me and makes people around me puzzled.

Thank you for your advice and honest words. I am not interested in general study. I would like to take the challenge and directly enter into the Master of Divinity course. God is so gracious.

YH: When I was attending the Iliff school of Theology, in my second year, I was required to do a Christian ministry internship. My placement professor said that I shouldn't do my internship at Denver Women's Correctional Facility because it will be difficult for me to be ordained if I do my internship outside of a church. I told him I will take care of that and asked him to just sign the paper and he listened to me. I didn't have any problem with the ordination process. Not just my husband but also one of my professors tried to discourage me from going into prison ministry.

I am glad that the Lord gave me the courage to say that I will be responsible for it and God took care of everything. So, please don't listen to others who don't think you can do it or it's because you are a woman or for any other reason. I am glad you understood what I was trying to explain. Have a good night.

Grace: I am glad that you are sharing your experiences with me. I treasure it because your study was also your journey with Jesus. I am excited that I will experience Him and His power more than before because studying is challenging and out of my comfort zone. I think that is a God given desire in me, and it is not a luxury, but a mission. In people's eyes, it is luxury; an ordinary woman takes a master course without having any clear career opportunities. However, it is not a luxury; it requires courage and sacrifice. I hope it also has an impact on many people in the future.

I planned to join the Culinary Program mainly to feed my pleasurable desire. You are right; that is a luxury. I will try to focus on Him rather than what people say and think.

6/9/16

YH: We have no time to waste. I've waited a long time so I just wanted you to know that as much as we are dedicated to the Lord, He will reveal to us that much. God led my studies. I believe He is leading your studies. You are right! Preparing for God's work takes courage and sacrifice. I am so glad that your husband is behind you. Have a blessed day!

6/14/16

YH: I am glad that you can translate the stories of *Women Who Lead.* I will be working on responding to your reference questions. I am proud of you for pursuing a higher education for the Lord and to use your gifts to the maximum for God's glory.

6/15/16

Grace: God sent you into my life; having someone who is successfully pursuing His will is a breakthrough in my life. I am so grateful for the Lord. He is faithful!

YH: We can depend on God. The other day, the Lord reminded me of my prayer: "Lord, if you called me to the ministry, prove it to me by providing money for school." He did it again with my Doctor of Ministry program. Praise God! As we decided to live for the Lord, things may be tough in some areas, but the Lord will show us that we are on the right path.

Grace: I will also ask Him to show me some confirmation about my further study.

6/16/16

YH: As you listen and get closer to Him, He will share His heart and more. It's good to have a question and to receive an answer from Him. Keep praying and you will get the answer. In the facility, I ask people to count the days they are praying for a specific prayer request and see how many days He will make them wait to give them an answer. Have a blessed day.

6/19/16

Grace: I've read your reference letter for my school. I've never received that kind of compliments. I will do my best to live up to the letter by being a humble,

Spirit filled, and well-equipped servant leader. In fact, I am still wondering where and whom I can serve because it is an entirely new road, so I asked the Lord to strengthen my faith. The Grace in the reference letter is actually the person I want to be. I think you have the mind of a visionary. That's why you can see ahead. I am glad that the Holy Spirit is always encouraging.

I like the book *Women Who Lead*. It was good and inspiring when I read it at first. Now, I see how much richer it is. I hope it will be an abundant blessing to the Korean society. Good night!

YH: I am so glad that you liked my reference letter. I will enter it as it is since you didn't say anything about correcting or adding. I can tell you that this is truth. God sees so much good in you more than anyone. What I see in you is just a little speck so just be ready. God can do so much more and that's why when we have the desire to serve and we should prepare to serve.

God will open the doors wide for you as you try to follow and obey the Holy Spirit. The harvest is plentiful but the workers are few. This morning, the Lord reminded me of the words He spoke to me at the beginning of my prison ministry. "I am looking for people that I can trust with my power to transform other people's lives."

These are the words He spoke to me in 1999. It's true that the Holy Spirit can work with those who paid the price. I learned that the price is high. I have to be humble, listen to the Lord, and obey the Holy Spirit. This is a test. A test to see if you will stick with Jesus and follow and serve him even through tough times. He wants people who can completely trust in the Lord and not their wisdom and understanding. Jesus is opening the door for you to go forward so you can serve Him with your gifts and talents. Praise God!

While I am writing this, the Lord asked me to ask you to gather all our conversations for the book, *Callings*. If you can't, it wouldn't be a problem. This book will help others who are seeking God's guidance on understanding callings. What many people struggle with is they lack direction in life even when they become Christians. *Callings* will challenge and guide them to discover how to follow their calling. It will help many young people especially women who need more role models to discern how to follow the Lord and use their gifts. What do you think?

Grace: Another amazement! I thought about keeping the emails from you because I've experienced a breakthrough while being coached by you. I mean learning how to listen to God's voice and how to be led by the Holy Spirit. The Holy Spirit told me many times to keep and organize the emails, but I didn't take it seriously. However, I am quite sure that I have all of them. I will try to find as many as I can, organize them and send them to you.

I hope the book *Callings* will guide and help many people arise for His Kingdom. I had everything in my life but I wasn't happy without knowing God's given task for my life. You wouldn't believe how pessimistic I was about life. I feel like I wasn't a believer in some perspectives. I was pessimistic, at the same time, pleasure seeking because I was blinded about the calling from the Lord. I don't know why I couldn't find it. I guess one of the reasons is that I didn't have enough people who were willing to coach me and patiently walk two miles with me in Matthew 5:41 "If anyone forces you to go one mile, go with them two miles."

I know my task now and I am so full and supremely happy. I still can't believe it is real. Knowing my calling has made a huge difference in my life, more than a difference. It's already changed my destiny. I wouldn't exchange it for anything. I guess I can complete the translation by the end of the month. Right off the bat, I will focus on organizing the emails and send them to you.

6/20/16

YH: Praise God! If God hadn't told me that He has given you the heart of a missionary and asked me to invite you to Colorado, I wouldn't have done it. In fact, the Lord is very clear on how I spend my time and how I mentor others. The Holy Spirit leads my time and He always reminds me of the words He spoke to me. "You are not doing it. I am doing it." I wasn't quite sure how He was going to lead me in the *Callings* book, but He is leading it.

With all the work, the Lord has made an impact on other people's lives through books. He helped me to write books throughout my ministry. It is not coming from me, but it is the Lord's leading and it's a blessing. After all, it's God's grace that He has called me to ministry and He has given me the opportunity to serve Him. I praise Him for that. You are right. Many people don't understand their calling. I was one of them. I didn't have a clear direction in life and wasted precious time so I ended up in wrong places. We can find our calling and purpose only by searching God's heart.

God has plans for each one of us. Only in God will our calling be clear as we try to listen and obey Him. Only then can we find complete joy and contentment and satisfaction. To understand our calling is a blessing. The Lord is willing to speak to us but many are not willing to listen. The Lord told me to teach others first how to "Love God," and second, "How to listen to God's voice." When we focus and practice on loving God with all our heart, mind, soul, and strength, we will be hearing God's voice.

Many people don't know how to love God so our conversations will be a natural way of explaining what is important in life and how God can bring healing and direct our lives so we can glorify God in all we think and do. People struggle because they don't understand their calling. I believe that's why the Lord is asking me to write, *Callings* to help others. We can find answers from God and people need to be reminded of it. I already entered your school reference. I added more to the section listing your gifts. I added "writing" as one of your gifts since it is true and I forgot to mention it. I am glad that the Lord brought you into my life. You have been a blessing to me.

6/21/16

Grace: I am so glad that I can contribute even a small writing for people. I hope it will be a source of celebration; as long as we live according to God's calling, life is a party. I believe the greatest gift in human life is knowing the Savior and one's own calling.

YH: Praise God! I thank God for calling me to the ministry. It's the most rewarding, fulfilling vocation I've ever had. I loved computer work at the beginning but that didn't fulfill my heart. My joy only lasted while I was learning new things. After that I got bored. However, knowing God, understanding His great love and power through ministry brings joy and fulfillment. This is something I've never experienced in any other vocation.

I understand what you are saying: "I believe the greatest gift in human life is knowing the Savior and one's own calling." Those who have experienced God's love and also serve Him understand the Joy of knowing Jesus' love and the joy of serving God. Welcome to the road of "striving to love and follow Christ all the way as we serve Him." Even in this life, I believe it is possible to live a life pleasing and honorable to Him if we are faithful all the way. I am so glad that we can work on the *Callings* book.

6/22/16

Grace: Lynette's story in *Women Who Lead* was the hardest project for me. So far it is the most heart-breaking story to me. I will keep on praying that the Holy Spirit will speak to the readers. I am still amazed!

YH: Hi, Grace, I am so amazed at how fast you can translate the stories. That's a gift. There is no way I could do it that quickly. Praise God that He gave you that gift and you are using it to glorify Him. Thanks.

I met with Lynette yesterday. She does most of all the book covers but now she is traveling more, so she is not going to make any more book covers for TPPM. I have all the files from her on a disk and I will be learning how to make the book covers.

She tried to help her mother but her mother kicked her out of her life. So, when she thinks about her mother, she is disturbed. She told me what helped her was before she goes to sleep, she imagines that her mother is in front of her and she would say, "Mom, I love you. I love you." She keeps saying this hoping that her mother's spirit can understand her love for her, since Lynette can't visit her mother. This also helps her sleep better. Instead of focusing on negativity, she focuses on loving her mother.

Lynette is one of the most loving people I've ever met. She helps many people. She helped me tremendously when I was working on my dissertation. She has a Ph.D, and told me it took ten years for her so she is very happy that I finished my dissertation in three years. That's because I have someone like her helping with my papers and many others working hard to help me. It's God who put the amazingly qualified and willing people around me to help me with my schoolwork. Praise God! He asked me to finish it and He helped me to finish it.

Lynette is writing a book but she told me her writing is becoming more like meditation and she thought when she finishes it, it will help inmates and she may donate it to TPPM. I am glad that you are excited about the book *Callings* and I think that's what I would like to talk about when I give a presentation to young people in December at Pastor Lee's church. I am glad the Lord is leading me to reach out so I can work on training young people.

I am so glad that you are translating these stories. I thought we already had many wonderful stories but

Lynette's story is powerful. I feel honored to know and have her as my friend. She didn't come to TPPM when you attended the TPPM celebration but Lynette has been a big part of my ministry. Why was it so difficult for you to translate this one? Again you did a great job of describing her story. Thank you for all your hard work. This book will bless many.

Grace: It's so helpful to know about your friendship with Lynette. I desperately needed to hear about a healthy relationship. "When we are closer to God, we can have truly blessed friendship..." It is a profound message. This generation is isolated, lonely, and many people are searching for genuine and heart-warming friendships.

Thank you for the question, "Why was it so difficult for you to translate this one?"

Lynette's story tells me many things about my family life. Codependency is a sickness and a deadly disease, but it is often shown as sacrificial love. It is a deception, foolishness, and devil's scheme to exploit one's life.

My grandparent's marriage on my mom's side was exactly the same as Lynette's parents. When I was three years old, I saw my grandma beat my grandpa out of rage. My grandma left her family when my mom was very young and my mom had to take care of her three younger brothers. My grandpa was a businessman who didn't spend much time with his family. My grandma gave birth to another man's son, gave the boy to his father and came back to her family ten years later. At that time, my mom had already been married to my father when she gave birth to me. My grandparents babysat me and I saw firsthand my grandma's anger and emotional instability. When I was three or four years old my grandpa left the family out of frustration. No one knows where he is.

My mom had a relationship with my father and they got married one month before I was born. Their marriage relationship was much worse and more inhumane than Lynette's. I've seen various types of codependent relationships, and marriage breakdowns among family members due to severe abuse. I myself have been in counseling for years because of codependency. It was tragic.

Needless to say, Lynette must be good-willed, good-minded and loving. However, I am still angry with people who were victimized by codependent relationships. If the victim is a family member, it is more painful because the victim's family members also have to bear the consequences of their wrong choices. I struggled with being emotionally detached from people who are suffering in co-dependent relationships. I begged my mom to leave my dad, since I was twelve years old, but she was there almost for 40 years. Eventually, she divorced him in the crisis of a life-threatening situation. Some people say it is a generational curse, spiritual bondage or relationship addiction.

Dependency is ultimately a God-given need alongside with love, security and significance. We, human beings, must be dependent beings. Without God, we may become the victim of false dependency and false intimacy.

While I was translating Lynette's story I cried over twenty times because I know what she is talking about. I yelled at her, "You should have... you shouldn't have..." Thank goodness, she ended her marriage after 17 years. My mom was in a worse situation for forty years.

By the way, it is a common cliche that pain brings us growth and a better future, but it doesn't turn out like that without the Creator. My dad became an orphan when he was ten years old and was brought up in a relative's home. However, he named himself 'orphan' and took advantage of family members and some others. He has been saying his entire life that "I had such a difficult life." How he manipulates and controls people were poisonous, but by the power of God's love, I forgave him. I love my mom, and Lynette, but what happened to them shouldn't happen to anyone. I hope her story will release many people from dysfunctional and codependent relationships.

I am hoping that the book *Callings* is published as soon as possible. What an exciting scene; God's people find their callings and pursue excellence with joy. Many are invited, but few choose to answer the call for various reasons. I think one of the reasons is that they don't know that they are chosen or what they are chosen for. I am content these days.

6/23/16

YH: Thank you for sharing your heart. Now, I understand why you had a difficult time translating Lynette's story. All the tears you shed were the Lord's tears and the Holy Spirit's healing power working in you. I am sorry that you had to endure so much because of others' bad choices. I am so glad that the Lord encouraged Lynette to write her life testimony. Your own story of how God brought healing besides the book *Callings* will help many. I can assure you that all the tears you will be shedding will bring healing to others.

I don't know how much I cried while I was writing *Twisted Logic, The Shadow of Suicide,* but this book helped many others. The Lord used the story to open others' hearts and brought healing in them.

Your family story is a painful story but the Lord will use it for His glory and bring healing to many others. Not because of your families' tragic story but how He has brought healing into your heart and has given you an understanding of how others are broken and need healing from the Lord. The Lord can bring complete healing to a broken heart. Going through this painful process teaches us God's powerful love and forgiveness.

Unless we have God's heart to forgive, it's impossible to forgive. We justify our anger, resentment, and bitterness. It's great that you are willing to follow the Lord and in the process, more healing will come in your life and heart in many areas.

Once you said to me, "It is painful; I am indignant from bearing the consequences of their wrong choices. Am I self-righteous?" I believe it's not self-righteous but it's "righteous anger." The Lord doesn't want us to dwell in anger, hate, or bitterness. It's hard to forgive someone who hurt our loved ones when abuse is continuous. I believe God understands. However, our attitude shouldn't be hating them enough to kill them but rather hoping that they would or will change. We need God's grace and a forgiving heart. That's my interpretation but the great examples of forgiveness go beyond our understanding or circumstances.

Stephen at the moment of his death sees Jesus and he prays, "Lord Jesus, receive my spirit." Then he fell on his knees and cried out, "Lord, do not hold this sin against them." When he had said this, he fell asleep." (Acts 7:59-60)

At the cross, Jesus said, "Father, forgive them, for they do not know what they are doing." (Luke 23:34)

Our attitude toward people who are sinning and doing horrible things should be to ask the Lord to forgive them even though we may not be ready to forgive them. Understanding where they are is important in forgiveness. Jesus knew that these people didn't know that he was the Savior of the world.

The Lord will lead you and bless you beyond imagination as you closely learn to follow and learn to love Jesus. He is your closest friend and your contentment comes from Jesus and I am glad that you are feeling that contentment.

Grace: I've been thinking about my attitude toward my father this afternoon. I agree with you that I haven't been around him for over ten years, so it's time to stop dwelling on the past hurts. I see I don't have a fruit of repentance even though I repented for my unforgiving heart. I began to ask the Holy Spirit to lead me so I can bear the fruit of repentance and forgiveness. Otherwise, I will be attacked by the devil continually, and become a never-ending cycle.

I wanted my children to use their musical talents, so I pushed them very hard. One day, my son got sick and the Lord told me to stop. I repented my controlling behavior to my children. Since then I've done my best not to be overly involved with what they do. It gave me and my family freedom and peace. I think that might be the fruit of repentance, but the fruit of forgiveness is still vague to me. Making amends might be one of the steps. Well, I don't have many ideas in my head. I feel like it is too challenging for me. I desire to leave a godly legacy for my children instead of passing on unforgiveness. I want to be an example of forgiveness and let them enjoy the fruit of it. I had some rotten food on my plate from the past generation and ignorantly ate it. It made me sick and paralyzed. I don't want to make my children innocent victims of my sin. I want to keep on being led by the Holy Spirit.

YH: I agree with you that you don't need to focus on past painful events. I learned from my son. If I talk about any negative experience from the past, he would say, "Mom, let's not talk about negative things because it seems like we repeat the same story." And sometimes when I talk about how some people had a horrible thing happened to them, he would ask, "What is the positive out come of that horrible story?" We'd quickly focus on the lessons and positive aspects of difficult times. Our conversations focus on present and positive things. This actually helped our relationship and brought healing in our heart.

We tend to focus on hurts and pain more than we should. In fact, sometimes if we are not careful, we go too deep into our past painful experiences that can become distractions in our journey of loving and serving God. I am very proud of you. You are taking a step toward letting go of the past. TPPM has blessed me so much in that matter. I have met people who are visionaries and focus on serving God and all of them have a heart for prisoners. I thank God for them. I thank God for you. Even though we have only known each other for 8 months, mostly through email, I feel I know your heart because of our common interest in is our Lord, Jesus Christ. I pray that the Lord will bless you and surround you with many godly Christian people who can mentor you and give you wise advice when you need it.

6/25/16

Grace: I've been struggling to understand what the good servant of God looks like. Tonight, my problem is solved. The picture wasn't that complicated. Matthew 21:5 "Tell the daughter of Zion, 'behold, your King is coming to you, lowly, and sitting on a donkey... 9...those who followed cried out, saying: 'Hosanna to the Son of David! Blessed is He who comes in the name of the Lord!' Hosanna in the highest!'" I see myself as His donkey; how blessed it is!

Jesus is sitting on me and I see people giving Him glory, and exalting His name. I received the vision from my heart by faith. I can hardly describe my feeling right now; I am just overwhelmingly grateful for seeing that.

YH: That is a great vision. I am glad that the Lord is showing you what we should be doing. We just have to carry the message of Jesus to others with a humble and willing heart.

He has everything to offer and that's all we need to tell others. All the wonderful feelings the Lord is giving you by leading your path are because you are listening and willing to obey.

This morning I went to pray and the Lord told me

that I should print 10,000 copies of the Spanish *Journey With Jesus Books 1-4*. I planned to print 3,000, so I asked the Lord, "What about *Maximum Saints* book fundraising, we need funds for that too." That was one of the reasons why I was going to print only 3,000 copies of the Spanish book. He replied, "I will help you raise all the funds. You don't have to worry about my project."

The Lord is again reminding me that timing is not in my hands but the Lord's. What I am doing is not my project but the Lord's. This releases all the pressure and He has done many miracles before. I just have to be patient with how the fundraising goes. As the Lord told me before, "You are not doing it. I am doing it." This gives me the right perspectives. Certainly if everything was in my control, TPPM couldn't have grown this much. I am glad that He is in control of the project. That's how He led me to print the first 10,000 copies of the *Maximum Saints* book instead of 1,500 copies for only the Adams County inmates. We raised $20,000 for two Spanish books before and the Lord provided it all. I am excited to find out how God will provide the funds this time. If you can pray for this, I would appreciate it.

Grace: Thank you for letting me know about the financial need for publishing the books; it is a rare blessing to know that Jesus needs something to feed five thousand people. We don't see those situations often, especially in North America. PMPM mothers already decided to donate some money for TPPM every month. We think we can only give fives loaves of bread and two fish, so we assumed that will be $30 per person. However, the subtotal we can donate became a bit more than we planned.

6/27/16

Grace: I had a conversation with my husband. He said that most people actually don't know their calling – that is normal and don't have to know it. We just do our best for the Lord where we are, and that is enough. Sounds right. I don't know whether knowing one's own calling is necessary or not, but it was a serious matter and critical to me. I would have been a sinner against God if I didn't have a God-given task. 2 Samuel 11:2 says "One evening David got up from his bed and walked around on the roof of the palace. From the roof he saw a woman bathing."

David lost a sense of his calling and got bored with life. Eventually, he sinned against God. I was like David before I recognized that God has a unique calling for me. Being bored without a task is a dangerous sign for me as well. If I didn't recognize that I had some important tasks for His Kingdom, I would have indulged myself with fleshly desires and pleasure until now.

I think I have a strong tendency to be bold to sin and quick to ignore my conscience. However, the Lord is gracious. He gave me a sense of calling and purpose. Living life under the calling is productive and fulfilling. Moreover, I've been experiencing a sense of calling and having a task has been protecting against me from sinning and even cleansing my soul. I see people around me that know the Lord yet are sinning and becoming miserable like King David because they don't know what their callings are. How come understanding our calling is not emphasized in our Christian walk? We don't wait for the Lord patiently to know our calling. We just give it up too quickly. I believe finding our own calling is mandatory in our journey.

I am glad to hear that my son wants to know his calling. Hopefully, and prayerfully, I will be an example for him. I've been on this journey almost a half year. I was too far away to grasp it in the beginning, but it's getting closer and clearer in my vision these days. For a long time, I wasn't sure of myself and my life, but I am quite secure these days even though I've faced some opposition. Praise the Lord!

YH: Thank you so much for sharing. I am so glad that you are seeing what I am seeing. God has a very important task for you and for everyone. I pray that the book *Callings* will motivate and give others the desire to seek their calling in Christ. I am amazed by how you are making a great and positive impact in your family.

It's great that your son wants to know what his calling is. I pray the Lord will help him to find it. "'For I know the plans I have for you,' declares the LORD, 'plans to prosper you and not to harm you, plans to give you hope and a future. Then you will call upon me and come and pray to me, and I will listen to you. You will seek me and find me when you seek me with all your heart.'" (Jeremiah 29:11-13) I believe this Scripture is for everyone.

You wrote, "I believe finding our own calling is mandatory in our journey." I agree and I believe that's why the Lord asked me to write the book *Callings*. I started my first chapter and started gathering inmates' stories for *Callings*. I have been busy typing their stories. I am blessed to know how God is working with you and many others who are seeking their calling.

God is amazingly loving and if we are open to Him, He will share His heart and lead us.

I thanked God yesterday and today for asking me to work on the book *Callings*. I am inspired by many of the inmates' testimonies. If the Lord didn't ask me to write, I couldn't have known this joy. Many of the inmates' stories have lessons to teach us. They are responding to their call to serve God in the worst situation.

Thank you for your prayers and donation from PMPM. I was thinking, the Lord told me that my vision was too small when I first decided to order 1,500 copies of the inmate's book, *Maximum Saints Never Hide in the Dark*. So, I ordered 10,000 copies and the Lord provided all the funds. God has been stretching me in many ways especially through projects. He is doing it through the people who are listening to the Holy Spirit. As we try to obey the Lord, we will see many more miracles. TPPM is God's project and I am very happy that we are a part of it. Have a blessed day.

7/14/16

Grace: I like your story but I feel like you are God's successful case and a fortunate servant of God in terms of ministry. I see many ministers who are not productive in their ministry. Well... I want to be like you, who found the right path in Him. Thank you for the testimony!

YH: I have received a lot from the Lord and I know it. If anyone has experienced what I have experienced, they would all be in ministry. One of the most important lessons I've learned or accomplished in my ministry is to listen to the voice of the Holy Spirit and obey. If God didn't lead my ministry path, I wouldn't be who I am today. Then I had to make sure that neither success nor accomplishment was my focus rather just loving Jesus. Also, the Lord teaches me that He did all of that and I was just obeying his command.

When you attended the TPPM meeting, I typed 3 pages of what TPPM accomplished in 2015, and I was going to print it out to share with all of the TPPM volunteers. The Lord told me to put it away and told me to focus on Jesus who did all the work and remember Him and what He has done for us. That's why we, TPPM volunteers, for the first time, had communion in our celebration. Since then we have communion every time we get together. Remembering Jesus is my preaching focus these days.

God teaches me this important lesson even when at home. A few weeks ago, I put all the TPPM books on the top of my bedroom dresser. Every time I passed, I was thinking about TPPM's accomplishment. Focusing on the books can become God's competition, like sports that take lots of people's time and heart away from the Lord. The Lord didn't like it. He wanted me to remember who He is and what He did for me.

Finally, I put away all the books under the desk so they are hiding there. I can grab them when I need to. It just happened that Holly drew a beautiful picture of Jesus carrying a cross for me. That picture is on my dresser. It helps me to meditate on what Jesus went through to save the world. The Lord is telling me to remember Jesus and I have to keep moving forward and not look back.

Grace: I am so glad that many people are working together to finish the book, *Women Who Lead*. I had a great experience while translating the stories. The Holy Spirit led my words completely. A long time ago, I attended a conference and there was a guest missionary speaker who served in Gambia in Africa. He said he received a blue print for building a church. He had no idea about that, but kept on asking the Holy Spirit to lead him and eventually he built a church by His guidance.

I was afraid of going to school. I wasn't sure of my ability but I gained confidence and courage after the translation. I learned that I can rely on the Holy Spirit in study. In addition, I experienced many other things, and it wasn't a labor even though it required lots of effort. Actually, I've thought about not going back to school, but just translating and reading the books since it was really fulfilling for me.

You are right, listening to His voice is the source of blessings. If I followed my desire and took the Culinary Program this summer, I couldn't taste that joy. I've been praying that the Lord confirms me about going to seminary. Recently, I visited a church in my community. It was not encouraging. The worship was of a contemporary type, and focused on entertaining and pleasing people. If a church focuses on just worshiping the Lord, people seem to lose their attention – we lost the true meaning of worship. Churches seem focused on people and attendance rather than worship.

YH: Have you ever thought about which denomination can ordain you as a minister? That might be something to consider so you can have more ministry opportunities. It's good to check different schools and listen to the Holy Spirit.

The Lord guided me in choosing a school and which church I should attend as well. Listening is very critical in finding the right path and finding peace.

I don't think you will have any problems with school. I struggled a lot but I always asked others to help me. There is always someone who can help and I am thankful that I had seven editors when I went to school. Your English is great. You will do fine.

7/25/16

Grace: I was so thrilled with reading a part of the book, *Callings,* which clicked in many ways for me. It already has so many insights and revelations. I loved it even in the beginning. It will richly bless many people. I can go to that school, but strangely, I don't have conviction from the Lord. In addition, I didn't want to go there somewhere in my heart, so I began to pray again.

YH: I wasn't sure about your question of confirmation. Which one are you talking about?

1. Confirmation to go to school, or

2. Confirmation to go to the school you applied for?

I believe the Lord will lead you to where you need to go, which school and all that. He knows what's best for you. Timing is in God's hands but listening is very important and I am glad that you are trying to listen. I love God's sense of humor. God is telling your husband about your future ministry through a dream. A car represents ministry in my dreams and your husband got that in his dream.

I wish my husband had had that kind of revelation from the Lord. Then I wouldn't have had to cry that much and suffer from resentment when my husband didn't support my seminary education. I had to drive on icy roads in stormy weather, risking my life. Eventually, everything worked out fine. The Lord had lessons to teach me. He wanted 100% commitment to serve God and going to school was showing Him that I was willing to do whatever He asked me to do. As I look back, my driving time was my time with the Lord and I had lots of conversations with the Lord. So, I can't complain. Praise God!

God has given you a challenging situation. There were times everything was going wrong with my family except my ministry. That was the only thing that gave me comfort and encouragement. I believe your suffering and pain will mold you into a person who will understand God's healing power and also others' pain. You will be able to have more compassion to help others. God uses all our pain for His glory.

Your friend is translating *Journey With Jesus* into Chinese. I know God is leading it and actually, the Lord is promoting the book, *Journey With Jesus*. The Lord told me, "See, I am doing it. I am promoting my book." It's amazing what He can do. God told me to visit a Tongan church one Sunday and I met a woman lay leader there. I gave her the TPPM books and told her she can volunteer to translate the books if she can. Three weeks later the Lord told me to visit this church for the second time. The Lord said, "They are waiting for you." When I visited the church, the lay leader brought a notebook and showed me that she stared translating *Journey With Jesus*. She said, "At first, I just started translating the story. Then I became the girl in the story. Soon, Jesus was speaking to me and I was weeping."

Well, the Lord changed my stubborn heart while I was writing this book. That's why I made a decision to go into the ministry. The Holy Spirit is leading it.

Grace: I will keep it in mind; the Holy Spirit is leading me.

7/31/16

Grace: I don't like breaking down and crying, but I am these days. I thought it was a sign of weakness, but I realized it is strength to get to the next step. I didn't know that I needed it, but Jesus knew it and has blessed me to grieve. I will be released from loss and its heaviness, and I've been restored and refreshed.

YH: I believe the tears the Lord gives you are a sign that God is getting closer to you. You are feeling the presence of the Lord. It is a step closer to the Lord in your spiritual journey. It is a process of purification, and the Holy Spirit's presence working in our lives to understand God's heart. We have to go through the process of purification for healing. I cried for one year when I was resisting going into the ministry. After I made a decision to go into the ministry, I cried for people who didn't know Christ. Now my tears are for those who live in sin and don't even know it. So, welcome into God's presence and try to understand what the Lord is trying to share with you.

Grace: Amazingly, volunteering at TPPM ministry is rewarding. It is more than a paying job. God pays us on earth and in heaven also. Knowing God's economy is exciting.

YH: I have received more than I have given. I am paid more than what I have expected on earth by responding to my call to serve the Lord. Now, I don't feel like I have much to receive when I get to heaven since I already got paid and received more than I have put into. I am blessed.

Grace: Praise the Lord! I am glad to hear it. I am laughing now. I feel like I am seeing your excitement over what He did for you. I believe doing what He wants me to do is beyond compensation. I've also been rewarded with so much peace, joy, and intimacy with the Lord. It only can happen to someone who has obeyed Him. Thank you!

YH: You wrote, "It only can happen to someone who has obeyed Him." If Moses didn't obey his calling to deliver the Israelites, he couldn't have a close relationship with the Lord. God is faithful to those who are faithful. He has been telling me that again these days, "I am looking for someone whom I can trust with the power to transform other people's lives." It takes time for the Lord to trust us and He will keep testing us to see if we can be trusted. This trust will come only through understanding God's heart and obeying him. The Lord talked about David, "He is a man after God's own heart." "He will do what I want him to do." That's trust. Have a good night.

8/6/16

Grace: It was a privilege to read a part of the book, *Spiritual Distraction*, ahead of other people. There must be a reason that God blesses and encourages me with the book. I was amazed at His provision; we shall not lack. It is practical and profound in content. It reminds me of the verse in Matthew 10:16-17 "I am sending you out like sheep among wolves. Therefore, be as 'shrewd (wise) as serpents and innocent (harmless) as doves.' Be on your guard against men..."

I give thanks to the Lord for my being able to read the book, *Spiritual Distraction*. It is very helpful for me and with God's appointment for my future. God is so good; He equips us to be strong for the battles. While reading the book, I realized I've faced many kinds of spiritual distraction in my life, but I didn't know they were spiritual distractions even though they were sort of ongoing issues in my faith journey. I was particularly puzzled and passive when believers become distractions in my life.

Now, I know it can happen when the other party looks devoted to God, but is not God-fearing. Fear of the Lord is so important for us and for others' sakes, too. I couldn't discern the current issues in my life. I was passive in dealing with them. I often said to myself, "Just forget about it." However, the Holy Spirit told me while reading *Spiritual Distraction* not to give up resolving the issues in order to be an efficient servant of God.

The book mirrors the demonic force behind the scene in my life. It shows me not only how to discern the distractions in my journey, it also helps me know how to not be a distraction to others. I am so grateful for your authenticity to share what happened in detail. I am not exaggerating; it is a breakthrough and a mandatory book to read for all the people who want to grow in serving the Lord. Praise the Lord!

YH: This is the book I never thought I would be writing but the Lord has guided me through it. I wish I had known about spiritual distraction before I went into the ministry. Then I could have prevented many distractions. I am glad that this book is going to help others.

8/26/16

Grace: All of a sudden, my husband said that he is not supposed to support my schooling financially. He told me my calling is being a mother and a wife, not ministry. Well, he confuses me and makes me feel like I am not eligible to talk about my *Callings.*

The Holy Spirit showed me Hebrews chapter 11 this morning when I was praying, so I let him know mine is an act of faith. He said he has been seeing many people who didn't have seminary training serving God and ministering. He said straightforwardly I don't have any calling for the ministries. He suggested for me to be self-sufficient if I still want to go for the studies.

The school starts September 7th. If I need to earn money for school, then I'd better go back to the Culinary Program. The wages from that training are more than minimum wage. It is a funny situation to go back to the beginning. I will pray about it.

YH: The calling is coming from God. Your desire to serve God is a calling and many people don't recognize it as a calling. In fact, that's what I was explaining to others the other day.

My husband's desire to serve God was a calling, but others doubted his calling. He never heard a voice telling him to go into the ministry so he had a difficult time going through the ordination process. The Ordination Committee didn't think my husband had a call to be a minister.

My husband had a sincere desire to serve God. He was a gifted preacher and he told me he couldn't be happy with any other vocation. Ministry was his calling but others didn't recognize it. However, many of his congregation recognized his call because of his heart for the ministry and the gifts he had.

Ironically, when my husband heard about my clear calling from God, he didn't pay any attention to it. He would have been happy if it was someone other than his wife. In fact, he didn't even want to accept that I was called to the ministry. He only mentioned that he didn't want me to be a minister but wanted my support as a pastor's wife.

I am sure you will make the right decision on what you should do. Follow the Lord and the Holy Spirit's leading and you won't have regret. I am sorry to hear this just before you were ready to start school. Ask the Lord what He wants from you. If the Lord gave you the desire to go to school, you will know it.

I couldn't stay home but I had to go to school to respond to my call. I was dying spiritually at home. I had to make a choice. I am glad that I listened to the Holy Spirit. I will be praying for you and your husband. This doesn't disqualify you from writing a book on *Callings*. This experience can only show many people face when they decide to follow their calling to serve God.

One of my mother's regrets is that she wasn't able to serve God with her gifts of healing. When she prayed, people were healed. If she had support from her husband, my mother could have helped many people but my father didn't support her. In fact, he abused her because she was a Christian.

I will go ahead with the book with your email so please trust me on this book project. The Lord is testing you to see if you are truly committed or not. I believe you have a calling from God and you are already serving Him in many capacities. He said, "I gave her a heart of a missionary." He also told me to invite you to Colorado. I wouldn't have invited you if God hadn't asked me to. I trust the Lord has called you and we just have to pray that the Lord will help you in this time and also help your husband.

Thanks for sharing your heart. When I went to school, I was actually deeply in debt because of real estate business. The Lord provided all the funds for school. All my school expenses were paid by scholarship. I still suffered a lot financially after I graduated. Eventually, the Lord took care of all of it. I had to learn to trust and rely on the Lord. All the problems helped me to pray more and helped me to get closer to God.

Grace: My husband asked me, "Did you hear it from God? Did you? Ministry is not for everyone, but only specific people." I want to serve people with God's word and I have a desire to study at a seminary but I couldn't when I was in Korea. I didn't want to deal with my dad's verbal abuse and violence. It was a hidden desire in me for long time. It's better late than never.

I am excited to go back to school. At least, I am not going to have regret on my deathbed that I didn't take the challenge for the Lord. In addition, we can afford it even though we are not rich. God proved to us already that He will provide all we need. In my mind, it is an investment. Secondly, he said I was not equipped enough for ministries because I didn't have much hardship in my life. I pondered what he said and the Holy Spirit told me about Moses' life. He was a royal prince until age 40, but he willingly identified himself as God's servant and began to face hardships after that.

One third of the tuition fee was already covered by a financial aid scholarship, $1,300. Thankfully, we can afford for the rest of the fee $3,000 for the semester. It was one of the signs for me that the Lord has been leading me onto the path. It is strange. I can hardly see people who are positive about my decision to study at seminary. Anyway, God is in control.

8/27/16

YH: I have confidence that the Lord will provide everything you need for school. I believe you will not regret finishing your education. You are preparing to serve God to the full extent and God will honor you for it. Also, check out if you can work in a hospital as an intern chaplain or other places as an intern chaplain after you start school. This will help open the door for ministry opportunities. You will have more connections to find a paid position in the future.

Your husband may not see your seminary education as an investment, but it is. Most people who don't have education can't get a good paying job even in ministry. Not only school is necessary for your own preparation for ministry, but also others will see that you are equipped to do the work of ministry when you have theological education.

Grace: Thank you for your prayers. Last night, I prayed and cried, "Lord, You provided the school fees for me, not my husband. Fulfill my desire and I will do my part. I don't want to give my husband any financial burdens, but I depend on You Lord."

My husband came to me and told me that God told him to support me. I asked him again to make sure that he is giving to God and not me. He said he couldn't sleep last night because of a headache until he surrendered to God. God spoke to him and said that He was leading me onto the right path, if it is not now, the opportunity might not come back again.

Thankfully, God confirmed to him as well that my study is in His will. It is good to have another confirmation before I start studying. My husband has earned and handled all the money for the family. I feel very inadequate about myself. I've never earned money for my family or myself after I was married. Sometimes, I felt I was selfish to go back to school. Fortunately, he was positive about my plan to study. I think he was not sure of it in the beginning or he was doubtful about my decision. I am glad God dealt with the issues for each of us. In this matter, God is responsible and He is in the center of it. I don't have to feel sorry for my husband and he doesn't have to think that his support is an unnecessary sacrifice, but instead obeying God.

I think these are confirmations from God. I don't have to feel inadequate about myself anymore. I am in God's unconditional love and grace. I receive blessings and give thanks to the Lord. Thanks again for your prayers and I will do my best to do my part. God is gracious!

YH: I am so glad that the Lord is speaking to you and your husband. I have to tell you that I would have divorced my husband if it weren't for the Lord. I had to commute 430 miles one way to attend school. After I had a car accident on the way to school, my husband told me that he was going to move closer to Denver so I didn't have to commute. He changed his mind after six months. I was devastated. I was ready to divorce him. The Lord told me not to because my husband actually helped me in many ways including my school and my ministry preparation.

I felt like I was dying. That was the most difficult and disappointing time in my life. The Lord pulled me out of it by leading me to write a book, *I Was The Mountain.* He taught me not to rely on people but rely on God alone. I learned to let go expectations of what others can do for me. I learned to trust God in any situation. That gave me peace. In the end, everything worked out with God's help.

I am also glad that things worked out for you and your husband. God is truly good and I am so glad about your decision to go to school.

Grace: God is gracious and resolved all my issues before school starts. My son is very interested in the Holy Spirit. *Invisible Counselor* is perfect for young people. If they clearly know about the Holy Spirit, they will be more efficient in their ministries and greatly benefit from their personal faith journey. Amazingly, he has read the book *Spiritual Warfare* and then didn't talk about his nightmares any more. It was a serious issue for a while before he read the book. *Invisible Counselor* is powerful. There are so many books about the Holy Spirit, but this short book contains all the extracts of the Holy Spirit. Again, reading the inmates testimonies in the book are the icing on the cake. Thank you so much!

10/11/16

Grace: I've been struggling with finding a church and disappointment at the seminary. I expected to learn something godly and grow in faith more than before, but I don't see it yet. I've been reading *Spiritual Distraction* now. Pastor Kim and Yong's testimonies are powerful to me. I learned there is no hope in people, but always Jesus.

YH: I understand what you are going through. My seminary years were not always that good. I had to confront professors about their non-biblical teaching but the most important part and what I treasure is my prison ministry. The most fulfilling and exciting thing happened while in school was prison ministry. I organized prison ministry. The school provided a platform for my ministry. The only reason I went to school was to get all the qualification I needed to become a minister. I expected very little and I just focused on passing classes. Also that's what I did with my Doctor of Ministry.

Studying may not satisfy you completely so you might have to find some ministry to fulfill what's lacking in the academic setting.

Lately, I started studying about Satanism and learned what horrible things people do to themselves and others. Now I have more appreciation for spiritual leaders who try to lead people in the right direction. They are trying to serve the Lord and I have more respect for them now.

I believe there is hope when I see people who care enough to sacrifice for God's kingdom. You are helping me a lot, too, but another person I want to mention is Shahin, a volunteer for Farsi translator. She gives me hope. She has been struggling with cancer for as long as I known her. Even when she was going through cancer treatments she worked on translation. She has translated eight books so far and she told me she just started translating, *Dancing in the Sky.*

She is doing it for the Lord's glory to bring more people to Christ. I learned that she paid the typist $5 per page because she can't type. Each book has about 200 pages, so it cost about $1000. She hasn't seen any fruit of her work yet.

Shahin is critically ill but she has kept translating for the benefit of her own people. This really touched me. God said in Jeremiah Chapter 5 that if He can find only one person who practices justice and seeks the truth, He will forgive the whole city. It's because people like Shahin, some day there will be more people who will find hope in Christ.

The reason you struggle in the church is because it's not time for you to be fed by others but fed by God, so that in turn, you can feed others. When I visit different churches I compose sermons in my head as I listen to other people's sermons. I gave up on feeding myself through others a long time ago after I realized that I shouldn't expect others to feed me. So you might have to find a church where your husband can grow and you can be involved in leadership so you can teach others. Your spiritual hunger comes from the Lord. He is showing you what you need.

Yes, if we can teach others so they can be fed by Jesus, that will satisfy many who are spiritually hungry. School is the same way. Many of the classes are just academic and missing on spirituality so it can be discouraging. I didn't expect much so I focused on what I could learn. One of my friends who started seminary quit school. He was disappointed by education. There may have been many other reasons for him to quit. He is called to the ministry but he is not in full-time ministry because of his lack of education. We can be disappointed but we also need to understand that professors are trying their best with what they know. It maybe hard to find qualified professors but we can learn lessons even in negative situations.

As I was writing this, the Lord reminded me of how He leads me. When I am discontent, the Lord has something to say. I usually stop talking and ask the Lord, "Is there anything you want to say to me?" So, maybe listening to God will clear your way - or give you directions on how to handle disappointments and discontentment.

Discontentment in my spiritual life is God is trying to get my attention. He has something to tell me or redirect my path. I will attach Bill's story from the book of *Repentance* to encourage you. This is a first draft so It needs lots of editing, but it will give you an idea of what the story is about.

10/13/16

Grace: I will stop grumbling and focusing on how

the Holy Spirit leads me. I have the same heart; I'd like to go back to translating the book. I will let you know how it goes. I am still happy to be at school

YH: When you have time, you may want to go onto the website and watch "Satanist to God." I had to pray a repentance prayer after I watched it. It's horrifying what people are capable of when they don't know God. Thanks for sharing. Keep up with your good work. Did you have time to read the story of "Bill?"

Grace: Yes, I read his story, but have not finished it; I am so grateful for his courage and efforts to write his testimony. The book *Repentance* is what we desperately need. I will start translating the book *Invisible Counselor* today. Thank you for your help. If I didn't read Stephanie's and Bill's story, I would have been in more distress. It is amazing how God orchestrates the things!

YH: God is good!

Grace: I finished reading *Spiritual Distraction* now. Again, it's amazing! It has so much wisdom and insights. God wants to give us freedom and function as His servant. Thank you so much. The book answered so many questions for me. Praise the Lord!

Part Four:
How to Respond to a Call to the Ministry

How to Respond to a Call to the Ministry

There are people who are called to be ministers of the Lord. They may be called full-time or part-time but they know they are called to serve Him. Whether you are serving God as a minister or as a lay minister, it is critical that you make a decision to follow the Holy Spirit's leadership in every area. I have been counseling many who want to serve the Lord and become ministers. The following are what I usually tell them to do so they can be prepared and equipped to follow their call to ministry.

(1) **Find the church** - Find a church where the spiritual leader is able to teach you so you can grow in the knowledge of the Bible and you can develop a close walk with the Lord. If the Pastors and other spiritual leaders love the Lord, use their gifts to serve the Lord and live a godly life, then you will be able to grow spiritually. If not, they can become a spiritual distraction in your own spiritual journey. You may be discouraged instead of encouraged to grow in faith. Pray and ask for

the Holy Spirit's guidance on selecting a church. The Lord knows where you should be. Listening and obeying the Holy Spirit's leadership is very important in selecting a church so the church can help prepare you to respond to your call.

(2) **Find a pastor or spiritual leader who can mentor you** - If you want to respond to the call to serve, you need a mature Christian mentor to mentor you. It depends on who is available to mentor you; you can use your gifts to the maximum or minimum. If you don't have a good mentor, you might be discouraged and not pursue your ministry path. In fact, some people may discourage you from using your gifts. They may think you are not qualified to serve. You need to find someone who has spiritual discernment so they can mentor you. It's critical to find a mentor who can hear God's voice as well so they are able to help you to prepare to be a minister.

(3) **Find a ministry where you can use your gifts** - Find a ministry in the church where you attend or if your church doesn't have ministries where you are called to serve, you might need to look outside of your church to find something you are called to do. Try to serve God with your gifts and don't give up when you can't find the right ministry. Keep trying and praying and the Lord will lead you. Your mentor can help you recognize your gifts as well.

(4) **Find a Bible college or seminary for theological training** - Education for biblical and theological training is necessary if you want to be a spiritual leader. Without education, many people won't think you are qualified or trained to be a spiritual leader, pastor, or minister in any capacity. You will lack credibility with them. There are

some churches that ordain people to be a pastor even though the person doesn't have any biblical or theological training, but that's rare. The problem is when they go to other churches, they will ask about their education. Education is necessary for people who want to be a spiritual leader. It shows their commitment and dedication to excel in everything they do in studying the Bible.

(5) Find a church or denomination where they ordain people - If you want to serve God as a spiritual leader but don't want to be a minister, you don't have to go through the ordination process. Ordination is a process for those who feel they are called to the full-time ministry. Full-time ministry allows a person to have another vocation but their ministry is their main focus. To do that it's important that you find a church or organization that will ordain you as a minister.

Conclusion

These are only guidelines for people who want to be spiritual leaders but always remember the three basic callings I mentioned in Chapter One: loving God, using our gifts to serve our neighbors, and living a holy life which brings God glory. Without being faithful to these three callings, our spiritual leadership will hinder others' spiritual growth. Becoming a spiritual leader is not for our own benefit but only for God's glory and to benefit God's kingdom. We have received many gifts and skills from the Lord. We are to use them to respond to Jesus' call to make disciples of nations and teach them to obey the Lord.

"Then Jesus came to them and said, 'All authority in heaven and on earth has been given to me. Therefore go and make disciples of all nations, baptizing them in the name of the Father and of the Son and of the Holy Spirit, and teaching them to obey everything I have commanded you. And surely I am with you always, to the very end of the age.'" (Matthew 28:18-20)

Responding to the ministry is a way of using our gifts to glorify God and help others who need God. In the process, we learn to follow the Holy Spirit and we will be growing in our walk with the Lord through obedience. Responding to our calling is following Jesus all the way.

He said, "Then he said to them all: "Whoever wants to be my disciple must deny themselves and take up their cross daily and follow me. For whoever wants to save their life will lose it, but whoever loses their life for me will save it. What good is it for someone to gain the whole world, and yet lose or forfeit their very self? Whoever is ashamed of me and my words, the Son of Man will be ashamed of them when he comes in his glory and in the glory of the Father and of the holy angels." (Luke 9:23-26)

Part Five:
My Story of Calling by Yong Hui

My Story of Calling
by Yong Hui

I personally reflected on my spiritual journey according to three callings that I have mentioned in this book: loving God, loving my neighbors by using my gifts, and living a holy life. It is God's grace that He had a plan for me so I can be a minister and learn these three callings and what's important in life.

Before I made a decision to go into the ministry, I didn't pay attention to these three callings. I didn't have a deep love for Jesus even though I believed in God. I didn't have love for lost souls, so I didn't have any desire to share the gospel even though I believed that unbelievers would go to hell. I didn't get into trouble with the law but I certainly did lots of things that God wouldn't approve of. I didn't have a clear understanding of the Bible so I was following worldly desires of loving money and being selfish.

The church gave me the foundations of faith but it didn't teach me how to love God. Because of that, I even backslid when my husband was ministering to churches. I only attended church on Sunday and I didn't take the time to read the Bible or work on developing a close relationship with the Lord. This led me to fall away from the Lord. I even doubted if God was real. This lasted 13 years and the Lord brought me back to Him by reminding me that the times I was fired up for the Lord were when I was reading the Bible. I was a Sunday Christian. I had something that was missing. I was not learning how to love God or using my gifts to serve Him to the maximum.

Therefore, in my teaching, I emphasize that loving God has to be an daily habit and every moment our focus must be to please the Lord and not be distracted by worldly desires. We have to discipline ourselves to worship God everyday, not just Sunday.

God called me to the ministry but I was resisting and tried to ignore my calling. Then the Holy Spirit led me to spend ten percent of my time in prayer, read one of the gospels out loud to learn about Jesus, and listen to the voice of God instead of just talking to God in prayer.

My final decision to go into the ministry came when I was writing the book *Journey With Jesus.* While writing this book, I realized two things that changed my heart forever; Jesus not only has love for me but He has a great love and compassion for the lost, and it's not my power but the Holy Spirit's power that will transform people's hearts.

I knew I didn't have the power to change other people's lives and I thought I had to do the work by myself. This was a misconception. All I have to do is obey the Lord when He asks me to do something. The Holy Spirit will do the rest.

The Lord had told me He had some kind of ministry for me. After I made a decision to go into the ministry I asked the Lord what He wanted me to do. The

Lord answered my prayer as He reminded me of what happened to my older brother. When my alcoholic father started beating my mother, my older brother ran away from home and became homeless at the age of 13. He got involved in gangs and was incarcerated three times in his teen years.

Visiting my brother in prison was heartbreaking for me. The second time I visited him, I was flooded with tears and even when I was called to see him, I couldn't stop my tears. My brother loved me so much and it hurt him badly. He said, "Why did you come?" I left that place in tears and never went back. It was too painful for me to see him there. I thought if we had a loving father, my older brother would never have run away from home and he wouldn't have gone to prison.

Then the Lord reminded me of another thing while my brother was incarcerated. I wanted someone to introduce Jesus to my brother. That never happened and my brother still is not a Christian. The Lord told me, "Go, tell them that Jesus died for their sins and the Father has forgiven them. Go and treat them like your brother." That's how God called me to prison ministry. He asked me to do what I wanted others to do for my brother.

God opened the door to prison ministry for me during my first quarter at the Iliff School of Theology. After reading my story *Journey With Jesus,* inmates from Pueblo asked Chaplain Lola West to come and share my testimony at their facility. I was so blessed by this visit that I organized prison ministry at school and went to eight different facilities with students.

The Holy Spirit is opening people's hearts in prison and revival is happening. After I graduated from

Iliff, the Lord opened the door at Adams County Detention Facility so I started working as a chaplain there in 2003.

My book ministry started while I was at Iliff and I published two books with a help of another prison ministry volunteer. Korean people donated funds for the printing of *Journey With Jesus* after they read the manuscript. I have seen firsthand the needs and effects of the book ministry. Once I started working at ACDF, I felt even a greater need for more books for inmates. They have the time to read and have fewer distractions. There are not enough books to go around, especially Christian books. The Lord continuously blessed me with book projects after we started Transformation Project Prison Ministry (TPPM) in 2005.

TPPM was going to print 1,500 copies of the first inmates book *Maximum Saints Never Hide in the Dark* but the Lord told me my vision was too small. So, I ordered 10,000 and the Lord provided all the funds. He continuously provides the funds so we can reach out to the prisoners and homeless with books that aid in bringing them to Christ.

These books are distributed for free and the Holy Spirit continues to use them to help many people grow in faith. I praise God for the vision He has given me and others who are volunteering for this project.

I never expected that book project to grow into what it is now. Translating books into eight different languages was not in my plan but the Lord made it happen. I thank the Holy Spirit's leading in not only my prison ministry to inmates, but also the book project through the many volunteers and donors who have become sponsors.

As I reflected on how I worked on responding to my call to ministry I realized the following:

First, I attended church all my life but my calling didn't come from the church teachings, instead coming from my personal prayer and Scripture reading. I was saved at home while I was reading the book of Romans and I made a decision to go into the ministry while writing *Journey With Jesus.* The Lord guided my ministry path.

The churches I attended somehow didn't encourage me to find out what my calling was. They didn't encourage me to listen to the voice of God. The churches I attended didn't teach me much about of the Holy Spirit. I didn't know how the Holy Spirit worked in Christian's lives. It was the Holy Spirit who taught me to listen to the voice of God through prayer, Bible reading, and listening in silence.

Second, finding a spiritual mentor was difficult but there was one Korean pastor who encouraged me to attend Suwon Bible College when I was in Korea. His influence was God's grace. He was the only one who tried to encourage me, other than my mother, who has been a spiritual mentor all throughout my life. She, however, didn't encourage me to go into the ministry because I am a woman. She didn't expect much from me; it was a cultural thing. However, after I made a decision to go into the ministry, she supported my decision and I believe her prayers are what helped me in my ministry.

After the Lord led me to start TPPM, many people became my mentors and supporters for my prison ministry and book projects. I trust these people and I feel I have many spiritual mentors who understand my passion and support me with prayers.

Third, God clearly called me to the prison ministry. I was able to use my gifts and I am so pleased with all the ministry opportunities I have through ACDF and also the book project. I just can't believe how much the Lord has blessed me with ministry opportunities. At the same time, I have to be careful to guard my time so ministry doesn't become my first love, and keep focusing on loving God. Ministry is loving my neighbors. I have to make sure I spend time with the Lord to understand His heart so I can develop a close and loving relationship with Him.

Fourth, the Lord blessed me with a seminary education and even a Doctor of Ministry degree that I didn't ever expect. There are many others who don't have that privilege. I know it was God's grace that I was able to have a higher education. In fact, I didn't need a Doctor of Ministry degree but the Lord told me that He was answering my prayers. I prayed that the Lord would use me to the maximum for His glory. By providing a full scholarship for all my education, the Lord blessed me with schooling so others would have no question about my qualifications to be a spiritual leader. I am very thankful for God's provision in this.

Fifth, my husband was a United Methodist Church (UMC) minister so I started the ordination process with the UMC. It actually worked out great. The UMC ordains female ministers and they have many scholarships to help women, especially ethnic women. I received my largest scholarship from the UMC and also one from the Iliff School of Theology, primarily because of my prison ministry.

As I reflect on my calling, the Lord blessed me by calling me to prison ministry. I wanted to see revival in America and the biggest revival I see is happening among prisoners. I am thankful that the Lord has given me the desire to write and guide me. Not only through my writing, but also through inmates' writings of transformation, TPPM is able to help many people.

The book projects blessed me so much more than I ever imagined. I can boldly say that I know God called me into the ministry to bless me. I was born to be a minister. It is the most fulfilling job I've ever had!

Appendices

An Invitation

Do you have an empty heart that doesn't seem to be filled by anyone or anything? God can fill your empty heart with His love and forgiveness. Do you feel your life has no meaning, no direction, no purpose, and you don't know where to turn to find the answers? It's time to turn to God. That's the only way you will understand the meaning and the purpose of your life. You will find direction that will lead you to fulfillment and joy. Is your heart broken and hurting, and you don't know how to experience healing?

Until we meet Christ in our hearts, we cannot find the peace and healing that God can provide. Jesus can help heal your broken heart. If you don't have a relationship with Christ, this is an opportunity for you to accept Jesus into your heart so you can be saved and find peace and healing from God. Here is a prayer if you are ready to accept Jesus:

Prayer: "Dear Jesus, I surrender my life and everything to you. I give you all my pain, fear, regret, resentment, anger, worry, and concerns that overwhelm me. I am a sinner. I need your forgiveness. Please come into my heart and my life and forgive all my sins. I believe that you died for my sins and that you have plans for my life. Please heal my broken heart and bless me with your peace and joy. Help me to cleanse my life, so I can live a godly life. Help me to understand your plans for my life and help me to obey you. Fill me with the Holy Spirit, and guide me so I can follow your way. I pray this in Jesus' name. Amen."

Transformation Project Prison Ministry (TPPM)

The Transformation Project Prison Ministry, a 501(c)(3) non-profit organization, produces and publishes books and DVDs and distributes them to prisons, jails, and homeless shelters free of charge nationwide. TPPM produces *Maximum Saints* books and DVDs containing transformation stories of inmates at Adams County Detention Facility, in Brighton, Colorado. Your donation is 100% tax deductible. If you would like to be a partner in this very important mission of reaching out to prisoners and the homeless or want to know more about this project, please visit: www.maximumsaints.org. You can donate on line or you can write a check address it to:

Transformation Project Prison Ministry
P.O. Box 220
Brighton, CO 80601

Facebook: http://www.facebook.com/tppmonline
Email: tppm.ministry@gmail.com

Transformation Project Prison Ministry is started in Korea. Contact: Rev. Lee Born, Director of TPPM
변화 프로젝트 교도소 문서 선교 지부장: 이본 목사
Website: http//blog.daum.net/hanulmoon24
Inchon-city, Bupyong-Gu, Bupyong 6-Dong 636-59
Heaven's Gate Church
인천시 부평구 부평 6동 636-59 하늘문교회, 이본 목사

About The Author

Yong Hui V. McDonald, also known as Vescinda McDonald, is a United Methodist minister, chaplain at Adams County Detention Facility (ACDF) in Brighton, Colorado since 2003. She is a certified American Correctional Chaplain. She is the founder of Transformation Project Prison Ministry.

Education:
- Suwon Presbyterian Seminary, Christian Education (1976~1979)
- Multnomah University, B.A.B.E. (1980~1984)
- Iliff School of Theology, Master of Divinity (1999~2002)
- Asbury Theological Seminary, Doctor of Ministry (2013~2016)

Books by Yong Hui:
- *Journey With Jesus, Visions, Dreams, Meditations & Reflections*
- *Dancing In The Sky, A Story of Hope for Grieving Hearts*
- *Twisted Logic, The Shadow of Suicide*
- *Twisted Logic, The Window of Depression*
- *Dreams & Interpretations, Healing from Nightmares*
- *I Was The Mountain, In Search of Faith & Revival*
- *The Ultimate Parenting Guide, How to Enjoy Peaceful Parenting and Joyful Children*

- *Prisoners Victory Parade, Extraordinary Stories of Maximum Saints & Former Prisoners*
- *Four Voices, How They Affect Our Mind: How to Overcome Self-Destructive Voices and Hear the Nurturing Voice of God*
- *Tornadoes, Grief, Loss, Trauma, and PTSD: Tornadoes, Lessons and Teachings—The TLT Model for Healing*
- *Prayer and Meditations, 12 Prayer Projects for Spiritual Growth and Healing*
- *Invisible Counselor, Amazing Stories of the Holy Spirit*
- *Tornadoes of Accidents, Finding Peace in Tragic Accidents*
- *Tornadoes of Spiritual Warfare, How to Recognize & Defend Yourself From Negative Forces*
- *Lost but not Forgotten, Life Behind Prison Walls*
- *Loving God, 100 Daily Meditations and Prayers*
- *Journey With Jesus Two, Silent Prayer and Meditation*
- *Women Who Lead, Stories about Women Who Are Making A Difference*
- *Loving God Volume 2, 100 Daily Meditations and Prayers*
- *Journey With Jesus Three, How to Avoid the Pitfalls of Spiritual Leadership*
- *Loving God Volume 3, 100 Daily Meditations and Prayers*
- *Journey With Jesus Four, The Power of The Gospel*
- Complied and published *Tornadoes of War, Inspirational Stories of Veterans and Veteran's Families* under the Veterans Twofish Foundation.

- Compiled and published five *Maximum Saints* books under the Transformation Project Prison Ministry.
- *Restorative Justice, Grace, Forgiveness, Restoration, and Transformation*
- *Restorative Justice, Reasons for TPPM's Grow of the Project and Motivation of the Volunteers*
- *Spiritual Distraction and Understanding*
- *Callings, Finding and Following Our Callings*

DVDs:
- *Dancing In The Sky, Mismatched Shoes*
- *Tears of The Dragonfly, Suicide and Suicide Prevention*

Books translated into Spanish books:
- *Twisted Logic, The Shadow of Suicide*
- *Journey With Jesus books 1-4*
- *Maximum Saints Make No Little Plans*

Books translated into Korean books
(한국어로 번역된 책들):
- 『예수님과 걷는 길, 비전, 꿈, 묵상과 회상』
  (*Journey With Jesus, Visions, Dreams, Meditations & Reflections*)
- 『치유, 사랑하는 이들을 잃은 사람들을 위하여』
  (*Dancing In The Sky, A Story of Hope for Grieving Hearts*)
- 『꿈과 해석, 악몽으로부터 치유를 위하여』
  (*Dreams & Interpretations, Healing from Nightmares*)
- 『나는 산이었다, 믿음과 영적 부흥을 찾아서』
  (*I Was The Mountain, In Search of Faith & Revival*)

- 『하나님의 치유를 구하라, 자살의 돌풍에서 치유를 위하여』(*Twisted Logic, The Shadow of Suicide*)
- 『승리의 행진, 미국 교도소와 문서 선교 회상록』 (*Prisoners Victory Parade, Extraordinary Stories of Maximum Saints & Former Prisoners*)
- 『네가지 음성, 악한 음성을 저지하고 하나님의 음성을 듣는 영적 훈련』 (*Four Voices, How They Affect Our Mind*)
- 『하나님 사랑합니다, 100일 묵상과 기도』 (*Loving God, 100 Daily Meditations and Prayers*)
- 『영적 전쟁에서의 승리의 길』 (*Tornadoes of Spiritual Warfare, How to Recognize & Defend Yourself From Negative Forces*)
- 『예수님과 걷는 길 2편, 침묵기도와 묵상』 (*Journey With Jesus Two, Silent Prayer and Meditation*)
- 『우울증과 영적 치유의 길』 (*Twisted Logic, The Window of Depression*)
- 『하나님 사랑합니다 2편, 100일 묵상과 기도』 (*Loving God Volume 2, 100 Daily Meditations and Prayers*)
- 『예수님과 걷는 길 3편, 영적인 여정에서 위험한 함정들』 (*Journey With Jesus Three, How to Avoid the Pitfalls of Spiritual Leadership*)
- 『자녀들의 영적 성장을 위한 지침서』 (*The Ultimate Parenting Guide*)
- 『멀고도 험한 길의 회상집, 미 육군 유격대 리키의 이야기』 (*The Long Hard Road, U.S. Army Ranger Ricky's Story with Reflections*) 리키 라마와 이영희 지음 (Ricky Lamar and Yong Hui V. McDonald)
- 『전쟁의 폭풍속에서, 퇴역 군인들과 그 가족들의 회상록』 (*Tornadoes of War, Inspirational Stories of Veterans and Veteran's Families*)

- 『용서의 기쁨』
  (Maximum Saints Forgive)
- 『예수님과 걷는 길 4편, 복음의 능력』
  (Journey With Jesus Four, The Power of The Gospel)
- 『용서가 낳은 치유의 은혜』
  (Tornadoes, Grief, Loss, Trauma, and PTSD: Tornadoes, Lessons and Teachings—The TLT Model for Healing)
- 『하나님 사랑합니다 3편, 100일 묵상과 기도』
  (Loving God Volume 3, 100 Daily Meditations and Prayers)
- 『평화를 찾은 사람들』
  (Tornadoes of Accidents, Finding Peace in Tragic Accidents)
- 『세상을 이끄는 여성 리더십』
  (Women Who Lead, Stories about Women Who Are Making A Difference)

"As Jesus was walking beside the Sea of Galilee, he saw two brothers, Simon called Peter and his brother Andrew. They were casting a net into the lake, for they were fishermen. 'Come, follow me,' Jesus said, 'and I will make you fishers of men.' At once they left their nets and followed him. Going on from there, he saw two other brothers, James son of Zebedee and his brother John. They were in a boat with their father Zebedee, preparing their nets. Jesus called them, and immediately they left the boat and their father and followed him." (Matthew 4:18-22)

"Jesus replied, 'No one who puts his hand to the plow and looks back is fit for service in the kingdom of God.'" (Luke 9:62)